The Role of the Non-Executive Director
in the Small to Medium-Sized Business

The Role of the Non-Executive Director in the Small to Medium-Sized Business

John Smithson

First published 2004 by
PALGRAVE MACMILLAN
Houndmills, Basingstoke, Hampshire RG21 6XS and
175 Fifth Avenue, New York, N.Y. 10010
Companies and representatives throughout the world

PALGRAVE MACMILLAN is the global academic imprint of the Palgrave Macmillan division of St. Martin's Press, LLC and of Palgrave Macmillan Ltd. Macmillan® is a registered trademark in the United States, United Kingdom and other countries. Palgrave is a registered trademark in the European Union and other countries.

ISBN 1–4039–3298–0

This book is printed on paper suitable for recycling and made from fully managed and sustained forest sources.

A catalogue record for this book is available from the British Library.

Library of Congress Cataloging-in-Publication Data
Smithson, John, 1946–
    The role of the non-executive director in the small to medium-sized business / John Smithson.
       p.   cm.
    Includes bibliographical references and index.
    ISBN 1–4039–3298–0
    1. Directors of corporations.   2. Boards of directors.   3. Small business.   I. Title.

    HD2745.S57 2003
    658.4′22—dc22   2003060852

10   9   8   7   6   5   4   3   2   1
13 12 11 10 09 08 07 06 05 04

Printed and bound in Great Britain by
Antony Rowe Ltd, Chippenham and Eastbourne

This book is dedicated to my best friends – my wife and my three daughters – without whose support and encouragement I would probably not have acquired the experiences in the first place, not have bothered to write them down, and not have persevered in the process of finding a publisher

Contents

Foreword

A few years ago I was asked to give a talk to a group of would-be non-executive directors about what was entailed in the practical side of operating in such a role. I decided to split the talk into two parts: in the first part I discussed what various 'authorities' prescribed as the requirements for a non-exec in terms of what you should be and what you should do, and then in the second part I went into some detail about what I had done and seen others doing in situations I had met during the course of my work – either as a consultant or as a non-exec on the boards of a number of small and medium-sized businesses.

The general reaction to what I said, and in particular to the differences I highlighted between what conventional wisdom claimed and what real life brought, made me think there might be some value in developing further the material I had prepared for my talk. Then, some time later, I took part in a research study which looked into the links between competencies and non-exec performance, and was struck once again by what appeared to be a difference between theory and practice. It seemed to me that a major element was an essential difference between what people from large organizations were saying and what those from smaller organizations were saying, and that herein lay the nub of the problem. Most of the available literature was clearly oriented towards what happened in larger organizations, and listed companies at that, and while there was much that was relevant and valuable there was a clear 'gap' when it came to practical handbooks for those specifically involved in SMEs in the unlisted sector. I began to suspect that there was perhaps such a book lurking somewhere in my experiences and the lessons I drew from them, so I decided to follow my hunch and try to put it together.

So here it is. It's personal, in the sense that it is based very much on what I have done, and what I have learned, in various roles as both a management consultant and a non-executive director; but it's also intended to be more generally relevant and to be of some practical use to those who are concerned in one way or another with providing non-executive input into small and medium-sized businesses. Although the context is very much that of 'corporate governance' as defined over the last few years by the various inquiries and reports from Cadbury onwards, it must be remembered that, as I noted above, most published material relates principally to large companies listed on the Stock Exchange, and it is very much these organizations that are expected to follow the precepts of Cadbury, Greenbury, Hampel, and, most recently, Higgs. My references to any of these reports will therefore tend to be general rather than particular. Furthermore, my focus is specifically on companies in the UK. I am aware that a fair amount of research and thinking has been done in relation to independent directors elsewhere – for example, North America and various western European countries – but all my own director appointments have been exercised within the UK, and hitherto I have not examined in any detail the possibility of comparisons arising from differences in national characteristics, company and associated legislation, and so on. Perhaps that would make an interesting future study.

I'm pleased to acknowledge the helpful material I have received from, principally, the Institute of Directors, PRO NED, and 3i, and the (sometimes unwitting) help and advice which fellow-directors – both executive and non-executive – have given me in organizations with which I have worked. I am also especially grateful to Margaret Williamson of Boardroom Development Ltd for allowing me to use material from her survey of non-Executive competencies, for generally encouraging me in the production of this book, and for reading and commenting helpfully on structure and drafts.

Finally and most importantly, I would like to thank my wife, Jane, for her help and support while the book has been in gestation, for reading drafts and helping to prevent some of the worst howlers I might otherwise have committed, and for putting up with me hogging the computer for hours at a time when I'm sure there were things she wanted to use it for.

One further point. The majority of company directors are men, and that applies both to executives and to non-executives. In fact, I have met several women directors, and a few years ago I took part in a project aimed at encouraging more women to become non-execs; and I have no doubt that, over a period, the boardroom will become less and less a male bastion, and rightly so. In writing about people, however, one comes up against the English language's gender differentiation in its personal pronouns, and I have to be honest and say that usages like 'he/she', 'his/hers', and (even worse) 's/he' often tend to strike me as contrived and slightly patronizing. So I will use only the masculine form in this book. If that upsets anyone, I'm sorry. But if it does upset someone, I think that person – male or female – is rather missing the point of the book.

JOHN SMITHSON

Introduction

Until relatively recently, nobody told you how to be a non-executive director.

To be fair, the animal was not all that common, and when it was encountered, it was usually in large corporations and tended to be part of a quasi-incestuous process whereby the great and the good operated a kind of swap-shop: the chief executive of group A would sit as a non-executive on the board of conglomerate B, and so on. This at least had the advantage that such people knew what was entailed in being a director, even if they might not (at first, at any rate) fully understand what a non-executive role should be. It was also sometimes used as a way of 'kicking someone upstairs' when they had reached their sell-by date as an executive director but couldn't realistically be got rid of – perhaps because of their large shareholding in the company, or perhaps for dynastic reasons – and right up till the early 1970s you might find people with grand-sounding titles like company president, vice-president, vice-chairman, and so on, whose presence could be inferred by the proliferation of zimmer frames each time there was a board meeting but whose actual contribution to the running of the company was negligible. The fancy titles didn't mean a lot, and in reality the individuals concerned might not fulfil any recognizable role as directors, but their names continued to appear in the annual reports and it no doubt made them feel good.

In smaller companies, these kinds of things didn't tend to happen. Owner–managers would often go on until they dropped – or until, sensibly, they sold out before dropping became a real and strong probability. In the meantime most of them would be unlikely to see any real benefit in having an outsider on their board, unless for some reason they had a pressing need to tap in to some specialist expertise and found that their solicitor or bank manager was a useful chap to have around on an as-required basis. Even in medium-sized businesses it was relatively uncommon to find any recognition that a formally-constituted non-executive presence on the board could add value in any meaningful sense.

It was possibly the emergence of 'popular capitalism' in the 1980s which changed the scene. The Thatcher government promoted wider ownership of company equity, and practised what it preached by making it relatively easy for individuals (who might never previously have so much as dreamed of becoming shareholders) to acquire shares in the various public utilities which were being privatized. There is almost certainly room for some debate as to whether or not this proliferation of equity owners was overall a worthwhile exercise in itself, but one beneficial effect was to remove some of the mystique from share ownership and make ordinary people realize that there was a role for them in this area. And partly because the range of shareholder interests that required to be protected was now becoming so wide, the means by which this protection was provided and underwritten – that is, by a strong and effective non-executive presence at the top of the organization – itself had to become more organized, more formalized, more 'professional' in the sense of widely-recognized codes and standards. In some instances, this process went as far as the setting up of national committees whose conclusions and pronouncements assumed a status almost akin to that of statute (of which, of course, more will be said later in this book).

At the same time there was an explosion in new company formation – this was no doubt partly due to the waves of redundancies which were an inevitable result of the shake-up which went on in British industry during that period, but it may well also have been partly attributable to an increasing feeling that there was now a culture in which entrepreneurship might flourish and in which it was no longer sinful to make money from commercial activity. Many new businesses were formed as buy-outs or spin-offs from former companies which had been either closed down or taken over, and in order to help to raise the necessary funds there was a tremendous growth in venture capital activity. This in turn led to an increased awareness of the phenomenon of the non-executive director, and to the perception that some codification of the role would be worthwhile. For how else could a substantial but absentee investor keep an eye on what was happening to their money? (This of course inevitably leads on to the question of the extent to which a non-executive may be perceived as a 'spy' or 'mole' for the investor: it is an important issue, but one which will be more appropriately addressed later.)

Some institutional investors appointed – and indeed many continue to appoint – one of their own staff as a non-executive director of an investee company, whilst others tended to opt for a more detached approach and preferred to appoint a third party as their nominee. Either way, it must have become clear over a period that there was a need to match horses to courses, and many of the organizations which accessed lots of non-executive directors became increasingly professional in the way in which they approached this. The main element of such an approach was to develop and use a properly organized resource base – in other words, if someone's only experience had been in multinational service companies it was probably wise to try to avoid putting him as a non-exec into a small widget-manufacturing business because he probably wouldn't make much of a worthwhile contribution there!

Thus from being a relative oddity, by the 1990s the non-executive director had become an almost essential part of a corporate structure, irrespective of the size of a company, and a cadre of non-execs began to develop across the country, with recognizable skills and with strong and increasing links with financial institutions. Even so, however, it wasn't – and indeed still isn't – easy to get a really good match between non-exec and company; and in particular the gap between large and small organizations has been and remains difficult to bridge.

There is an obvious gap between PLCs and private companies, of course, but there is also a significant gap – in culture, in method of working, often in calibre of people – between smaller and larger private companies. The SME – that is, Small to Medium-sized Enterprise – has become a recognized category of company, with its own identifiable characteristics and, more importantly, its own specialists. This book is predicated upon the belief (based upon extensive experience on the part of the author) that someone who is steeped in the culture and methods of a large corporation is not likely to be able to make a really valuable contribution to the governance of a small company. Indeed, it can be somewhat troubling at times to see early-retired big company executives hawking themselves round as potential non-execs of small businesses, whether under the guise of so-called 'business angels' or as would-be institutional nominees, or simply as bog-standard non-execs touting in their own right. Whilst obviously some of these people are extremely competent and valuable, regrettably others can sometimes do more harm than good.

But who else is going to fulfil the role? If someone already has a job, especially one with heavy responsibilities which demand much in terms of time and effort, is it realistic, still less reasonable, to expect him to devote any time or energy to a non-executive role in another concern? Perhaps it's only the retired who are in a position to do this – and perhaps indeed it's only the retired-from-a-large-organization who can in fact take the financial risk.

Whatever the answer to that, and notwithstanding any reservations concerning absolute suitability, it is likely that many 'new' non-execs will get their first appointment (maybe their first few appointments) in small organizations, and it is obviously important that they understand what can go on in such places if they are to be effective and worthwhile. Although there is a greater availability nowadays of training, there is still something of a shortage of good material to help those who get involved in the small-to-medium-size sector. Books about management tend to be written from the standpoint either i) of the academic, who is likely to concentrate on larger organizations because they lend themselves more readily to case studies and are more easily accessed by those seeking information and/or opinion, or ii) of the successful manager who has been there and done that, who, if he has the profile to be a potential best-seller, has almost certainly achieved his success and his public standing in the context of a national or multi-national organization. Interestingly, many of the latter also tend to be predominantly autobiographical, and as such do not always seek to draw conclusions of a more general applicability – although honourable mention should perhaps be made of Sir John Harvey-Jones' book *Making it Happen*,[1] which manages to combine autobiographical narrative with what might be termed 'pronouncements' (albeit almost exclusively relevant to large, not small, organizations), and of Patrick Dunne's *Directors' Dilemmas*,[2] which although not strictly autobiographical is based on material and cases he witnessed and experienced in his role as head of 3i's Independent Director Programme, and has perhaps more – but by no means exclusive – relevance to small organizations.

Not only is there something of a shortage of good published material relating to small business, but in addition it is by no means certain that – despite much apparent lip service from government, media, academia, and professional organizations, and despite the herculean efforts of such bodies as the Federation of Small Businesses – the essential characteristics, needs, priorities, and vulnerabilities of SMEs are properly understood by those who advise, sustain, or harangue them! There appears to be an increasing realization now on the part of SMEs of the potential value of having a non-exec, but it is open to question whether this is yet matched by the level of realization on the part of non-execs of just how that value could or should be maximized.

Indeed, there is an argument that the contribution a good non-executive director can make is so important that the whole issue needs to be tackled a great deal more formally and seriously than has up till now been the case. The Institute of Directors has recognized this, and is actively preaching – and, to its credit, practising – the cause of training for non-execs. However, there is at least anecdotal evidence to suggest that although SMEs in particular do need the kind of input that non-execs can provide, all too often they don't get it because there isn't the resource to go round. And the reason why there isn't the resource to go round is because nobody has yet defined properly what it is that is needed and how it would best be accessed and applied. That is what this book will attempt to address.

I have been an active member of more than thirty boards of directors, and have acted in a consultancy capacity to at least a dozen others. In particular, over a period of some twelve years, I held non-executive positions in more than twenty-five SMEs, ranging in size from start-from-scratch businesses to established companies with turnovers in the range £5–10 million.

This all came about as the result of a decision towards the end of 1984, after some seven years with a major consultancy group, to go solo. Assignments for local enterprise organizations had led to a lot of involvement with business start-ups and small companies attempting to grow and to break out of the financial and operational straitjacket they seemed inevitably to find themselves in. On occasions, as part of such an assignment, there was a role that needed to be played in directly advising start-ups or would-be start-ups, and it was particularly striking to note the almost complete absence of any worthwhile *management* assistance available to them. There were grants, loans of various degrees of softness, premises on favourable terms, and so on, but nobody seemed to be able or willing to tell people *how to run a business*. Quite often, particularly in depressed areas where enterprise organizations were operating, there were 'clubs' of various sorts where owner–managers could go and meet, and some of these organized courses aimed at teaching aspects of management. Indeed, from time to time I myself delivered sessions on courses such as these, mainly to unemployed ex-managers who wanted to set up their own businesses.

But it wasn't lectures or seminars that people really needed. In any case, the unemployed were arguably the wrong audience anyway – the target should have been people already running, or just about to start running, their own business, but of course they were too busy to take time out to attend seminars. It really seemed to me that what a lot of these people needed was a 'tame' consultant on hand, but one whose experience was of real business, real problems, not one whose milieu was the panelled boardroom or the strategy conference. There were two main problems. One was fee rates: the sort of fees charged by most consultants were simply out of the reach of the new or small business, so realistically one had to be self-employed, or part of a small consultancy with low overheads, to be affordable. Secondly, most consultancy work tended almost by definition to be on a project basis – defined terms of reference, fixed timescale, pre-agreement on deliverables, and half-an-eye to the 'extension' assignment sale. This seemed to be only part of what start-ups and small businesses wanted.

Then an article appeared in a business publication describing how some small businesses had used non-executive directors as a kind of ongoing relationship-based resource, and this helped to crystallize the ideas that had been forming in my mind. By marketing to banks, venture capital houses, and so forth a combination of input as both a potential consultant and a potential non-executive director, aimed in both cases at start-ups and small companies that wished to grow, work was obtained under both headings.

The appointments arose from all sorts of sources, and were variously welcomed or resented in the relevant boardrooms. They occurred, too, in a wide variety of types of business, as well as in several different sectors, including the public and voluntary sectors (for they by now had also embraced the idea of having non-executive directors) and entailed learning things, and coping with situations, of a kind that might never otherwise have been dreamed of. In particular, it was noticeable how frequently the need arose to act in a 'company doctor' capacity, trying to put right things which threatened the very existence of the particular organization, while at the same time contributing to an ongoing team-based top management operation.

Occasionally it was possible to find seminars and courses to go on that had some relevance, occasionally it was possible to pick up useful bits of knowledge as a result of membership of various professional institutes, and of course occasionally there was valuable information to be gained from fellow non-execs at get-togethers such as those mounted by 3i's Independent Director Programme. But to a large extent it was a case of learning on the job. Consequently, this book is an attempt at distilling what was learned and, in effect, putting together something which might have been useful to me and others like me as a work of reference, had it or something like it been available!

The book is divided into two parts. In Part I there is an examination of what it takes, or what various people think it takes, to be a non-executive director, and an attempt is made to assess how relevant this is to SMEs. In particular, I shall look at some recent research and try to relate its findings to the views of established authorities in the field, offering comments where appropriate from personal experiences, some of which support, and others which contradict such views. In doing so, the aim will be to try to juxtapose practicality with accepted wisdom, and assess whether or not they seem to fit. Part II of the book deals with some specific case studies taken from my own experience of the way non-executive directors have impacted upon companies' performance. There will be an honest attempt to highlight successes and failures equally, identify reasons for these various outcomes, and assess whether any coherent conclusions may be drawn, particularly in the context of the principles discussed in Part I.

It should be stressed, however, that this is not meant to be a purely academic study. True, a certain amount of third party research will be looked at and evaluated, and a certain amount of original opinion offered. But overall, the book is an attempt to produce something of some practical use: i) to people undertaking positions as non-executive directors in SMEs and ii) to those appointing them or brokering such appointments. It is offered in the hope that those who read it may recognize themselves, and/or their situations, in some of the descriptions, and in either agreeing or disagreeing with the findings and opinions may perhaps be able to influence their contributions, and those of others around them, in the direction of good corporate governance.

Part I
Analysis

1
The Non-Exec's Function

The need for measurement

Between the early 1980s and the early 1990s, the proportion of PLCs with non-executive directors on their boards rose from around 50 per cent to over 90 per cent.[3] At the same time, smaller companies, and particularly private companies, were also increasingly appointing non-executive members to their boards, and as was suggested in the previous section it is perhaps logical to postulate that it was the increase in the role and significance of venture capital houses, as much as anything, which led to this taking place.

Those who nominated non-executive directors to boards seemed to have two main considerations in mind: the ability of a non-exec to make a positive contribution in some way to boardroom processes, and his function in, as it were, 'policing' those processes. The first of these has already been identified as a motivation for having a non-exec, and was quite probably what brought them into being in the first place, whereas the second was a rather more recent issue which was part of a wider trend towards scrutiny and transparency. For, in effect, a new 'climate' was developing, where the extent to which executive performance was objectively measurable and, indeed, objectively measured, was greater than ever before: non-executive board members were a very visible and substantial manifestation of this.

Then into this new climate suddenly erupted, in the late 1980s, the so-called 'fat cat' issue. This centred around a perception – gleefully exploited and exacerbated by the media – of company directors receiving excessive remuneration, or profiting excessively from the purchase and sale of companies. (It has occurred again, more recently, in relation to falling company performance and rising executive remuneration.

As with the previous manifestation, there is an underlying justification for the outrage but perhaps not for the extent of self-righteous posturing and specious indignation that it has given rise to.)

Feline obesity was in reality a quite separate and distinct matter, both in origin and in significance, from the 'climate' referred to above, though it happened to catch alight at around the same time. And because it also coincided in time, to an extent, with the expansion in venture capital-related appointments, it provided another kind of incentive towards codifying and strengthening the role of the non-executive director. This found its realization, as it were, in 1992 in the establishment and processes of the Committee on the Financial Aspects of Corporate Governance (the so-called 'Cadbury Committee').[4] The point should be made at this stage that the Cadbury Committee's focus was very much upon the large public companies, in which the perceived abuses had been happening, and did not really have the smaller company much in mind during its deliberations. Still, its influence and the implications of its output have pervaded even the smallest of boardrooms, and we underestimate its importance at our peril. Almost a decade later, Cadbury is cited whenever matters of corporate governance are debated and, in particular, whenever boardroom roles, responsibilities, and behaviours are under the spotlight. Subsequent to Cadbury, there have been further reports on various aspects of corporate governance, from Greenbury,[5] Hampel,[6] and most recently Higgs.[7] None of these appears to have had quite the impact of Cadbury, possibly because Cadbury was the first, but they have all given rise to great debate on corporate governance issues and have helped to ensure that the matter has not simply gone away or been forgotten. (In the case of Hampel and of Higgs, the recommendations are specifically intended for listed companies, whilst Greenbury too, although saying that his principles apply equally to 'smaller companies', sets out a code of practice to be followed by listed companies. The relevance of these reports, therefore, to the type of organization being looked at in this book, is more in terms of a context than of a model.)

So what are the essential characteristics of the function of a non-exec, and why should it appear to need the sort of codifying and strengthening referred to above? Is it in fact possible, and relevant, to distinguish between the function in large organizations and that in smaller ones, and does this have an impact on how effectiveness may be assessed? Indeed, can objective measures be applied to a non-exec's effectiveness, or does it at the end of the day come down to *perception* and the nature of the relationship between a non-exec and his colleagues?

There is in fact a very strong argument that such objective measurement is perfectly possible (as well as desirable); moreover, it is increasingly clear that objectivity of measurement can be extended into relatively intangible fields, such as relationships and organizational climate. However, scarcely anyone does it, least of all in smaller organizations, and that is an unfortunate and unsatisfactory state of affairs. Perhaps it is a function of the relative 'newness' of the whole notion, perhaps it is something to do with a failure to recognize when something is of real potential significance, perhaps it is nothing more than backside-covering – whatever, it ought to happen, and there isn't really a valid excuse for its absence.

Clearly, the Cadbury Committee thought it should be perfectly possible to apply some objective criteria to assessing the role and contribution of non-execs, at any rate in the field of corporate governance. But it is of course one thing to produce *ex cathedra* pronouncements from the vantage point of a committee room, quite another to look in practical terms at how real day-to-day life actually works, and at the kinds of situations non-Execs are called upon to face. The process of translating pronouncements into practicality has consumed much attention and effort since Cadbury, and it is sometimes not easy to distil the points of most relevance, particularly where the smaller business is concerned. The remainder of this chapter attempts just such a distillation.

Accountability and duty of care

Perhaps the best starting point, then, is a general consideration of the function of a director – that is to say, any director. As in so many fields which are regulated by law, there is a clear *duty of care*. All directors as such have a duty to exercise reasonable care and diligence, as well as employing their talents and skills, in the performance of their functions. They are expected to act honestly and in good faith, and in all their actions to safeguard the interests of the company and its stakeholders (that is, shareholders, creditors, employees, customers, and arguably those in wider society who are in some way touched or affected by what the company does). There are provisions in the Companies Acts, the Insolvency Act, and the Financial Services Acts which define and govern what directors ought to do, ought to know, and ought to make it their business to find out; and such provisions – and indeed the entire duty of care – apply no less to non-executive directors than to executive directors.

The way in which directors may be called to account, and indeed the whole legal framework which governs the conduct of directors, means that being a director is not the same as being a manager, although many directors will also have management roles and responsibilities in the particular organization. A manager's performance of his duty of care will, in all probability, ultimately be judged in the context of some kind of performance appraisal process, within and according to the procedures of the organization which employs him, whereas a director's may ultimately be judged in a court of law, and a criminal court at that – if you are in any doubt about that, you have only to think of the number of occasions when charges, arising out of accidents or disasters involving employees of an organization, or its products, or indeed just its property, have been brought against directors of the organization who were nowhere near the event at the time and who were not aware of, and made no direct contribution to, its happening. The *Marchioness* disaster[8] and the Lyme Bay tragedy[9] are just two relatively recent examples, but there are plenty of others. It is not unknown for such prosecutions to end in jail sentences, and with the prospect now of 'corporate manslaughter' charges being increasingly employed, this is surely likely to happen more and more. In a civil, as distinct from criminal, context, directors have to look over their shoulders at the DTI, whose powers in cases of insolvent liquidation are quite draconian (and, it has to be said, there is more than a whiff of Stalinism in the way in which they are exercised . . .) and can lead to the loss of a director's livelihood or even most of his assets. And, of course, even if such extreme civil or criminal outcomes are avoided, the damage done to a director's reputation by the attendant publicity may easily be so great that he finds it difficult to get work again afterwards.

So it is by no means only the more widely publicized types of cases such as 'fat cat' activities, share dealings at the time of mergers or take-overs, and so on, which serve as warnings that being a director is not something to be undertaken lightly – headline writers are quite capable of leaping at anything which shows directors in a bad light, and whether justified or not the impact can be quite devastating.

A non-executive director has by definition no operational or functional responsibility, but despite that he is no less accountable, and no less liable, than an executive director. Lord Newton, the Institute of Directors' professional standards director, puts it very neatly: 'UK company law does not see the [executive and non-executive] roles as different and therefore does not distinguish between their responsibilities.'[10] This has of course clear implications in terms of the need to be adequately briefed and informed, thrown into sharper focus by the fact that a non-exec does not have the day-to-day contact with what is going on that an executive will have. Section 214.2 of the 1986 Insolvency Act, for example, carries a clear message to the effect that a director's conduct in the event of a company trading fraudulently or while insolvent is related not only to what he should have known, but also to what he should have made it his business to find out!

In other words, therefore, it isn't sufficient for a director, be he executive or non-executive, simply to accept as given all of what he sees or is told – rather, he must take all reasonable steps to satisfy himself that he is in reality fully and properly informed about the conduct of his company's affairs. So one of the first priorities of a new non-exec on his appointment must be to familiarize himself thoroughly with the organization, what it does, how it does it, who its key people are, and what the major issues of the day are which may come before the board. At the same time, he also needs to establish procedures for obtaining regular information thereafter, and he must be prepared to make this a major issue of principle – if the company won't keep him properly informed, he should tell them that he won't serve on their board, and it's as blunt as that. It can be surprising how much weight a non-exec's attitudes can carry, especially if he is a nominee of a significant shareholder such as a venture capital investor, so when he and the company establish the ground rules for his directorship, at the time of his appointment, he needs to ensure that those ground rules include the satisfaction of his requirement for information.

So context, actions, and power all interact in helping a non-executive director to fulfil his duty of care. But what about the ethical basis on which a company operates? Here, too, there is a clear element of the duty of care. It could arise in a number of areas – for example, advertising and marketing policies, a company's attitude to the environment, its employment policies, and the way it behaves towards those who owe it money or those to whom it owes money. If a company is actively defrauding or misleading its customers or suppliers, or for that matter its shareholders or indeed the public at large, or is trampling underfoot the rights or interests of its employees or of third parties, the non-exec has a duty to raise his voice against this. If he does not, and the company is found out and publicly exposed – or even prosecuted – he as an individual director, even a non-executive, is in the firing line, and rightly so.

Non-executive and independent directors

It is worth noting, in passing, that sometimes a non-executive director is referred to as an 'independent' director. This may be just a question of terminology, and in various countries where attempts have been or are being made to draw up codes of conduct and practice for boards of directors there are all sorts of semantic arguments going on around terms such as 'independent', 'unrelated', and 'outside' which may variously be used to describe members of a board who are not them-selves integral to the day-to-day running of the enterprise. It is arguable that, at least in a British context, a distinction of sorts can in fact be made between 'non-executive' and 'independent' directors. The ven-ture capital company 3i, for example, which nominates a large number of non-executive directors to the boards of investee companies, has tended always to refer to them as 'independent' directors.[11] 3i's stance is that they regard 'independence' as an extremely important criterion – so much so that they will usually consider a person for a potential non-executive director nomination only if he has a significant degree of *financial* independence. The reason is fairly obvious: the less you depend on your non-exec appointment for your income, the less likely it is that you might be influenced by the personal financial implications of a particular decision choice. An emphasis on independence, in this context, isn't a case of 3i impugning an individual's probity, it's just sound common sense and, moreover, offers a degree of protection to the individual non-exec in the sense that it makes him less susceptible to improper pressure from other directors or interests within, or connected with, the business.

Clearly, however, that's not the whole story. 'Independent' could also mean having no financial connection, other than by way of a fee, with the client company; that is, not holding shares in it. The Cadbury committee recommended that non-executive directors should be 'independent of management and free from any business or other relationship which could materially interfere with the exercise of inde-pendent judgement'.[12] This actually goes a bit further than just having no financial connection, and would seem to relate on the whole (quite understandably, in the context of Cadbury's sphere of work) to larger companies rather than small ones. For in larger companies there may well be several directors who fit the above description – indeed it is by no means uncommon today for there to be as many non-executive directors on a large company's board as there are executive directors (and, if Higgs' recommendations are followed, there may well be a structure of some kind within the non-executive part of the board), and in such circumstances the very definition of 'independence' is quite important. The probability is that because in a small company there is likely only to be one non-exec, the issue of independence is likely to be more straightforward, though of course no less important.

So the matter of independence and the way it is to be defined is worth discussing in some detail, for it is quite clearly one of the crucial elements in any relationship between a non-exec and a company. For the present, it is sufficient just to put down the marker of its significance, but the issue will be returned to later when the key roles and attributes required of non-execs are discussed.

Areas of activity for non-executive directors

The directors of an organization – collectively – must concern themselves with certain specific areas:

- *strategy*: the overall aims of the organization and the broad way in which it must set about achieving them;
- *policy*: specific programmes and actions in terms of the organization's operations which will contribute to the overall achievement of the strategy;
- *resources*: the financial, human, and technical resources necessary to implement the policies;
- *performance*: the extent to which progress is made, through proper utilization of resources, towards fulfilment of policies and strategy.

Again, these are the proper focus of both executive and non-executive directors; the difference comes in the degree of involvement or otherwise in the operational aspects. It is likely than non-execs will be concerned primarily with the first, strategy, and with the last, performance (or, more particularly, performance review), and probably to a considerably lesser extent with the middle two, policy and resources. Most conventional wisdom supports the idea that a non-exec's prime focus is at the strategic level, and that it is inadvisable and unnecessary for them to get involved at any detailed level. This may clearly be seen to be the case in large organizations, where there is a management structure full of people whose very function is to be involved at detailed level; in a typical SME, however, such a structure will be at the very least a good deal thinner, and in fact quite possibly non-existent, with no discernible dividing line between the strategic and the operational. Indeed, it has been suggested that one of the dangers of an SME having a non-exec at all is that he might be unable to resist the temptation to get involved at a detailed operational level, and that the executives may themselves encourage the temptation. The potential this has for giving rise to tension touches on the central issue being written about here, so it will be returned to repeatedly during the course of this book.

Conventional wisdom seems also to suggest that in an SME, the prime role of a non-exec is most probably to augment the knowledge, skills, and experience of the full-time management team. In essence this is probably just about right, though it could well be taken a stage further insofar as there is frequently also a 'teaching' element in the SME non-exec's role, in terms of guiding the executive directors through a kind of transition between being 'managers' and being 'directors'. The best managers in the world won't necessarily make good directors, and indeed many of those who start up small companies haven't a clue about directorships, especially those who start up with what might be called an 'entrepreneurial' motivation (by which is meant that they want to be independent, to work for themselves, and to stand or fall by their own efforts rather than always having to work as employees, and cede control of their destiny to others). It is frequently the case that, even when some members of a board have previously been directors – for example, when some directors of a company have staged a management buy-out from that company and have subsequently become directors of the newly bought-out company – there is still a need to ensure that ground rules are laid down for distinguishing between someone's role as a manager and their role as a director.

Yet it goes wider than this. The right non-exec will also be able to bring an amount of business experience with him which is complementary to what already resides within the company. One of the shortcomings many SMEs have is that, perhaps because of the time commitment required of their people, they can tend to become rather narrowly-focused, unaware of what is going on in the world outside their door. It is frankly surprising (and not a little distressing) how little some executives in a typical SME know about other local businesses, opportunities, relations with local authorities, enterprise organizations, and so on, and in a number of cases a major part of the function of a non-exec in such an SME has to be to provide such an 'external dimension' to their thinking. Moreover, the fact of being independent of the company can mean that the non-exec doesn't need to be at all defensive about any deficiency on the part of the company or its activities, which in turn will often lead to a greater ability and readiness to look at fresh ideas, approaches, and contacts. Additional contacts such as those a non-exec can bring can be of enormous value, sometimes in terms of commercial opportunities, sometimes in terms of enhanced credibility for the organization. The former is a fairly obvious aspect of networking, but the latter can be of as much benefit although perhaps less directly – the fact of having an individual with a good personal reputation on its board can lend credibility, particularly to a small company, in possible market places or among possible professional helpers such as financiers.

There is undoubtedly an argument which says that at least some of the above could be achieved just as well by using external professional advisers rather than non-executive directors, but there are two compelling points against such a contention:

- the cost of an external adviser, who is likely to charge on a time-related basis and therefore to be limited in the amount of valuable input he can provide;
- the authority which is conferred on a non-exec by virtue of being a member of the board, combined with the responsibility which he willingly accepts and which arises from a commitment to shared objectives.

These are especially applicable in the case of SMEs. As far as costs are concerned, it is relatively uncommon for small businesses to engage outside advisers anyway unless they absolutely have to (for example, for audit purposes, or if for some reason legal advice is needed), for the cost is usually prohibitive – or, if you try to get an adviser on the cheap, you get an inferior one. As far as the importance of being a member of a board is concerned, the sense of teamwork in a board of directors is often more noticeable in a smaller environment, and in fact more crucial to the success of the enterprise. But more importantly perhaps, there is the statutory aspect to consider – an external adviser operates at arm's length and is likely to be nowhere to be seen in the event of, say, a receivership and subsequent report by the receiver on the conduct of the directors. Simply by being on a board, a director accepts his share of responsibility for the way the business is run, and his share of any possible legal exposure. This demonstrates commitment to the organization, and also gives the director an element of authority in what he says and does. It is sometimes necessary to put one's foot down very firmly if, for example (and yes, it does happen from time to time), a managing director wants to pursue a course of action which looks to be extremely dodgy and potentially of borderline acceptability to any

DTI inspector. It is quite in order to say words to the effect that, although you like him a lot and enjoy working with him, you aren't prepared to go to jail for him!

To see the non-exec as part of a team, rather than as an absolute outsider, is actually a very strong view to take, and one which is likely to optimize his contribution. It may be inconvenient to be phoned up at all hours by your executive colleagues, but it at least means that they attach a value to what they seek from you without necessarily counting the detailed cost. An 'ordinary' adviser (consultant, or whatever) is much less likely to be used in such a way because the fee-meter will start ticking as soon as the telephone is lifted.

At the same time, however, perhaps the key attribute a non-exec can bring is his objectivity, exploiting the absence of a management responsibility by standing back a little and taking a broader view of what is going on in the business. He is also less likely to be blinded by the 'aye been' syndrome ('this is how we set it up, this is how it's always been done since, it's been successful, so this is how we'll go on doing it...') and therefore more open to fresh ideas. Of course, the trick is that if he's recognized at the same time as being a committed part of the team then probably the executives will listen to what he says, whereas if he's perceived as a little *too* semi-detached they may be tempted to wonder what the hell he knows about it anyway.

The view of the agencies

There are several organizations which provide access to non-executive directors, among which it may be argued that the Institute of Directors, PRO-NED, and 3i are of prime significance. Each has its view of what a non-exec should be there for, so it is instructive to look at what each says on the matter.

The Institute of Directors strongly supports the principle of having a non-executive presence on a board, and itself offers a kind of 'brokerage' service to match directors to opportunities. The IoD states that:

> The role of the non-Executive Director, be it in a large multi-national or a small growing enterprise, is complex. At its most general, it involves bringing experience and expertise to all the work of the board. Much more specifically, the role involves playing a key part in helping ensure that the company is kept under control, both indirectly by the shareholders and directly by the board. It must

necessarily be seen in the context of the wide duties and responsibilities of the board of directors itself.[13]

This is a good start, so far as it goes, but although clearly valid, it is little more than a statement of principle, giving limited insight into what a non-exec should *do* in practice or into the qualities or abilities required. There is a need for a focus, a framework, within which to operate, and the IoD's pronouncement risks being long on rhetoric and short on practicality, doing nothing to suggest what that focus or framework might be. In fairness to the IoD, this may stem from the fact that, as a professional institute, it needs to relate to members in a huge range of types and sizes of organizations, and to find a form of words which embraces all its members and their host organizations. This means in practice sheltering behind generalities, rather as final communiqués emanating from high-profile international conferences do.

However, the IoD does subscribe approvingly to the Stock Exchange Combined Code,[14] which includes a code of best practice containing several specific comments (many owing their provenance to Cadbury, Greenbury, and Hampel, and in due course the code is likely to be updated post-Higgs) in relation to non-executive directors. Principal among these are:

- at least one-third of the members of a board should be non-executives;
- the majority of non-execs should be 'independent' (for a discussion on 'independence', see earlier in this chapter);
- a remuneration committee, and an audit committee, of a board should each consist entirely of non-execs;
- a non-exec's appointment should be for a specific period of time, and that re-appointment should not be automatic.

These items clearly inhabit the same world as that which was described earlier, defined by the Cadbury Report, the Insolvency Act, and so on. They don't relate very clearly or specifically, however, to small businesses, reinforcing perhaps the perception that the IoD is predominantly the voice from the top of 'big business'. Such a perception is unfortunate and possibly unjustified, given that 60 per cent of IoD members work for SMEs – perhaps, then, the IoD has some work to do in terms of its own PR! It is certainly the case that, for example, the preponderance of high-profile executives from large organizations on platforms at IoD conferences does tend to reinforce still further the big business perception, so although the IoD is now making much more of a 'play' towards the smaller end of the company size spectrum it does perhaps need to back that up increasingly with some real and tangible results (products, services, opinion, and so on) which can clearly be seen to be designed specifically and distinctly for SMEs.

Another perspective is offered by PRO NED. This organization was established in 1982. Originally sponsored by nine bodies interested in promoting the quality of company direction and management (The Bank of England, The British Bankers' Association, The British Merchant Banking and Securities Houses Association, The Confederation of British Industry, The Institute of Chartered Accountants in England and Wales, The Institute of Management, The Institutional Shareholders' Committee, The London Stock Exchange, and 3i) it is now a wholly-owned subsidiary of one of the leading executive search organizations in the world, Egon Zehnder International. For several years PRO NED's chairman was Sir Adrian Cadbury, later chairman of the eponymous committee.

Unsurprisingly, PRO NED has concerned itself with the issue of corporate governance, and has produced a number of sets of guidelines relating to the selection and performance of non-executive directors. These include a number of what are clearly extremely valuable observations, including:

- the importance of maintaining a sense of proportion and distinguishing between what it would be sensible and worthwhile for a non-exec to become involved in and what he should steer clear of;
- the utmost importance for a non-exec to establish personal credibility at an early stage in the relationship with the company, so that in times to come he will be listened to even when his audience doesn't like what he has to say;
- the primacy for a non-exec of matters of principle rather than of practice.

PRO NED's thoughts tend however – rather like those of the IoD – to be oriented towards sizeable organizations (which may of course have several non-execs on their board), and pay particular heed to the situations in PLCs where there is an overwhelming need for transparency in board proceedings arising from Stock Exchange rules and other statutory requirements. Consequently, although PRO NED's guidelines and opinions contain what could probably be described as 'universal truths' to which this work will happily make reference from time to time, they do seem to be very much based on a perception of the non-exec role which is much more easily related to large companies than to small, and therefore to be of associated, rather than direct, significance to the central thrust of this book.

Possibly the best description of what a non-exec should be and do, and also the one which has the most relevance to the small business, is one that was set out several years ago by 3i, in a booklet entitled *The Role and Contribution of an Independent Director*,[15] which at one time used to be given to individuals who were nominated by 3i to a company's board. It identifies five principal areas in which non-execs should expect – and be expected – to make a contribution, and these are worth quoting in full:

1. To provide practical and creative guidance to the directors and management of companies and support the Chairman and Chief Executive as a confidential adviser.
2. To have helpful views on securing the best use of boardroom time to ensure that sufficient consideration is given through the year to strategic and innovative matters and the maintenance and development of a strong executive structure.
3. To be involved with the management team in the creation of a robust policy and strategy and the plans and budgets needed for their fulfilment.
4. To give objective advice to the board on the company's performance and guidance on the principles of corporate legislation.
5. To bring outside experience relating to the financing and conduct of companies and contacts with third parties such as financial sources, customers, suppliers, and Local and Central Government Authorities.

As a comprehensive but succinct exposition of the role of a non-executive director, it is hard to see that being bettered.

The 3i booklet also makes a number of additional points, principal among which is that a non-exec must, to be effective, win the confidence of the key executive and become that person's natural adviser and confidant. It acknowledges that 'it takes a lot of time and effort to achieve this'.[15]

3i doesn't in fact say whether they relate all this to any particular type of organization – in terms of size, sector, or any other characteristics – and it is perhaps a measure of the quality of thought behind their code that on examination it may be found to have an applicability across a whole range of organization types. Over the years, 3i's portfolio of investments has covered an enormous spread of company categories and types, so it is perhaps logical that their observations about non-execs should be capable of being applied to an equivalent spread of types – even though increasingly nowadays they tend to be interested only in sizeable investments and have rather outgrown, as it were, their earlier involvement in relatively small-scale start-ups and management buy-outs. However, such a change in emphasis in no way undermines the validity of the ideas expressed here by 3i.

Non-execs in the public sector

It is interesting at this point to explore whether the universality of the 3i concept of non-executives' roles applies to the public sector as well as the private. For in the public sector, the introduction by the Conservative government during the 1980s and 1990s of private sector-type disciplines and modes of operation created, if nothing else, an awareness of accountability of a type that had not previously seemed relevant. It also introduced a cadre of management that related the concept and practice of added-value to both inputs and outputs – even though it may be strongly argued that that accountability and that added-value were severely compromised by a political agenda which was perceived (with some justification) as being inherently antagonistic towards the public sector as a whole. Notwithstanding this reservation, however, the idea of a significant non-executive presence in organizations delivering a wide range of publicly-funded services represented a radical departure from any previous thinking, and opened the door to a cross-fertilization of cultures and ideas which has, arguably, not yet run its full course and which must surely offer rich pickings to students of management theory and practice. Indeed, the public sector itself has begun to recognize this and to review its own practices in this area, with the work of the Commissioner for Public Appointments[16] being a major step in the direction of clarifying and regularizing what happens.

The key requirement for non-executive directors in the public sector appears to be their ability to exercise – and be seen to exercise – independent judgement. Since many of the organizations concerned are relatively specialist in nature there is clearly an essential function in being a 'bridge' between the organization and the general public, and in providing a disinterested focus on issues which might otherwise generate heat rather than light. But there is also an underlying requirement to represent the public-as-paymasters, a requirement which seems to be every bit as complex as that of representing a commercial investor, but perhaps even less clear in terms of the demands placed upon the representative.

Linked to this is another worthwhile function for such people as guardians against the kind of cynicism which seems almost inevitably to attach itself to public sector organizations – to provide a measure of openness and transparency which will hopefully reassure the public about what is being done in their name. As part of the effort in this direction, it is quite usual for the non-executive directors of a public sector organization to take some direct responsibility for matters of relations between the organization and the public. It is also usual for such non-execs to participate in proceedings within the organisation related to matters of professional competence, discipline, and so on.

On the face of it, the areas of activity described above are somewhat different from those set out by 3i – if anything, perhaps, more particularly focused, almost *complementary* to what is (presumably) being provided by the executive directors, whereas 3i's list could perhaps be seen as more *supplementary* in that apart from the final item about 'outside experience' it appears not to offer much that could be described as exclusive to non-execs. However, on closer examination it does become clear that there is a measure of compatibility between the non-exec roles in the private and public sectors, especially in the context of ensuring that things are done properly and are seen to be so.

But at the same time there is a need to take note of an argument which says that many public sector organizations are so specialized in what they do that there is only perhaps a limited value in having non-executive input unless it too is similarly specialized in background. Nowhere, perhaps, is this argument more strongly put than in the Health Service, where the reforms of the 1980s and 1990s introduced NHS Trusts to run acute hospitals and community health services, each trust being managed by a board on which executive directors were in a minority.[17] Not only that, but even amongst the executive directors the clinicians were in a small minority. This kind of arrangement provoked a degree of controversy at the time it was introduced, and a degree of resentment among clinicians. What the argument seems to boil down to is this: although it is undoubtedly legitimate to have administrators and accountants in the National Health Service to carry out and manage those functions, couldn't it also be true to say that actual decisions relating to the running of health organizations are not really a legitimate area for people with no clinical knowledge or, at least, background understanding to get involved in because of the specialized nature of the factors relevant to and bearing on those decisions? In other words, special pleading by any other name – horses for courses at an extreme.

It is worth giving this issue extremely careful consideration. It seems pretty fair to say that there is without any doubt a vast body of knowledge and understanding in the area of clinical theory and practice, and it takes medical students (who in terms of the 'A' level grades required of them for entry to university may be said to be among the brightest of undergraduates) five years to learn it and a working lifetime to keep up-to-speed with it. How can any outsider credibly claim to have any understanding of the issues involved in, for example, competing claims for priority from different clinical areas or specialisms, or the merits of different approaches to clinical management structures? Can a non-executive NHS director or trustee even hope to make any worthwhile contribution to a debate about resource allocation within an acute hospital, or between an acute hospital and a community facility, or between one client group and another?

But if this point of view is accepted, then two further points must inevitably follow. First, if those without specialized knowledge or experience are to be excluded from a decision-making process in a specific specialism, then decisions at NHS board level about human resources and personnel matters must be left entirely to the HR specialist director, those about finance to a qualified accountant, and so on – highly selective enfranchisement and, for that matter, disenfranchisement of directors! This is quite simply and self-evidently not practicable, nor is it even desirable; it makes a nonsense of any concept of corporate accountability and militates against sound decision-taking and, indeed, against effective overall management. The second point offers perhaps a way of over-coming that; if the sphere is indeed so highly specialized, then perhaps specialists (in the case of the NHS, clinicians) should form the decision-taking majority, rather than remain in a minority as at present. But to be realistic, would they in fact want to? The truth is, they probably wouldn't. Why undergo extremely arduous clinical training for several years and then find that a significant part of your job isn't actually clinical at all but is all about management?

Clearly, there is a balance to be struck here. There is a strong argument that management is a skill area, just as cardiac medicine or intensive care nursing (for example) are, and that some of the skills are not really transferable. Where there is a requirement for the application of specifically *management* skills, that requirement is in itself independent of the functionality of the particular organization – for example, balancing the books in a hospital requires the same skills as balancing the books in an engineering company or, indeed, in a corner shop; and dealing with HR issues crosses boundaries in a similar sort of way. Where the difference comes is in the bits and pieces represented by the figures the bookkeeper has to deal with, or in the types of work being done by the people who give rise to the HR issues. Advice usually is – or certainly ought to be – on hand to guide a manager through some of the technicalities involved in the issues he is being asked to tackle, and a suitably intelligent and perceptive manager should as a result be able to understand the issues sufficiently to be capable of arriving at relevant and worthwhile conclusions.

There is also a whole field of argument about policing, apparently at its sharpest relief when it comes to the professions. Self-regulation has on quite a lot of occasions been shown to be inadequate as a means of maintaining control and public confidence, and during the 1980s and 1990s there was something of a proliferation of 'Offs' of various kinds – Oftel, Ofwat, Ofgas, and so on – whose function was supposed to be to provide a safeguard against the perceived perils of unbridled enthusiasm in policy making on the part of the relevant executives, especially in the newly-privatized utilities. Various attempts were also made from time to time by government to regulate the professions, though without any real notable or lasting success. However, at least there was an element of success in getting some basic management disciplines installed in the way the professions ran themselves and their affairs, and it may be argued that the introduction of general management into the NHS in the 1980s (unpopular though it was with many health professionals) probably saved the Health Service from a descent into financial chaos.

So perhaps there isn't really a need to get too heated about this matter. The point has already been made – and indeed, it underlies the whole of this book – that there can be both good and bad 'fits' between non-execs and organizations in terms of skills, culture, background, and so on, and that this itself is a key issue that needs to be addressed. Indeed, the 'fit' may in fact be more important than the detail of a specific background. An effective non-exec may have identifiable qualities or identifiable types of experience, or a combination of both, and part of the aim of this work is to establish whether there is any 'universality' in what makes an effective non-exec. There is surely some *prima facie* value in having at the very least an element of relevance in the previous experience which a non-exec can draw upon, and it does appear that those who appoint or promote the appointment of non-execs think that way too, but there really does not appear to be much evidence of the 'special pleading' previously alluded to. Some non-executives have made extremely valuable contributions to the activities and progress of highly-specialized professional organizations, contributions which say far more about the non-execs' own personal qualities than about whether or not they have relevant sectoral experience. The relationship between horses and courses is quite a complex one, and the debate around it will be considered in Chapter 4. It does not, however, appear to offer any convincing grounds for excluding the public sector from consideration of the role of the non-executive.

Adding value

Indeed, if there is a discernible common thread running through all of what the IoD, PRO NED, 3i, and for that matter the government (or, more probably, their advisers) have to say, it surely lies in the concept of added value. Non-execs are of course absolutely entitled to expect to be properly remunerated for what they do, and therefore in the end they represent an additional cost factor. Nobody in their right mind would willingly incur additional cost for their organization without looking for a return which at the very least is going to neutralize that cost and preferably will more than make up for it, and there is no valid reason why such a philosophy shouldn't be rigorously applied to the role of non-execs.

This is particularly the case when the cost represents a significant element in the organization's finances. Possibly in a large PLC the odd £20K, or even £50K or £100K, in fees to a non-exec is no more than a minor blip in the profit and loss account and can readily be written off or absorbed somewhere or other; but in the typical SME the impact is likely to be much greater and more immediate. Suppose that a typical gross margin achieved by an SME may be somewhere in the range, say, of 25 per cent to 30 per cent – in that case, a fee of £10K to a non-exec (which isn't particularly generous but is probably reasonably representative) will take sales of £30K to £40K to recover before any additional (and hopefully consequential) profit is realized. Is the non-exec contributing positively to achieving that? If not, he shouldn't be there. And in the non-commercial sector, the question is in effect the same – is he manifestly and measurably worth the money they are paying him? If not, again, he shouldn't be there.

For, to return to the notion put forward near the beginning of this chapter, it is increasingly practicable to measure performance today, and to identify and apply criteria for recognizing success (or failure) and quantifying it. In a commercial context, there are the more perhaps 'traditional' measures of sales, profit performance, shareholder value, and so on; in the public sector, these might tend to be replaced by 'softer' items such as response times, outcomes, levels of complaints, and so forth. These are all measurable, they may all be affected by the actions of directors both executive and non-executive, and the causality may be quite specifically highlighted. More and more, hiding places for under-performers in the adding-value stakes are becoming harder to find.

Conclusion

It seems clear that the principle of using non-executive directors has now established some firm roots and in so doing has become increasingly accepted in areas where in the past there would have been neither understanding nor even perhaps awareness of what they were or what they could do. There is, furthermore, some clarity about the overall focus they should have – on governance, strategy, and so on – though as yet rather less clarity about the detail of how that should be put into practice. However, there is absolutely no suggestion that they are not relevant to any one particular sector, or to any one particular type or size of organization, and neither is there any real suggestion that they cannot form part of (and stand or fall by) a system of objective measurement of performance. It is therefore valid and realistic to claim that non-execs have a potential relevance and value to the smaller business. The next chapter will focus on the smaller business's particular characteristics and needs.

Summary of key points

- The increased use of non-executive directors coincided with awareness of, and reaction to, perceived abuses of the power and influence of companies' boards of directors during, in particular, the 1980s.
- The Cadbury Committee, which reported in 1992, was a recognition of the need to clarify and measure the role and performance of non-execs.
- Company directors have a basic duty of care and responsibilities which are underpinned by various statutes. This duty and these responsibilities lie no less on non-executive directors than on executive directors.
- Non-execs must satisfy themselves that they are fully informed about their companies and the ethical and practical basis on which they operate.

Summary of key points   (*continued*)

- Non-execs must be able to demonstrate a degree of independence from the company. This may include financial independence.
- Unlike a large organization, an SME is unlikely to have comprehensive management resources, and these may therefore need to be augmented at times by a non-exec's input.
- Although a non-exec's input may be similar to that which could be provided by an external professional adviser, there are advantages (in terms of continuity, cost-effectiveness, and commitment) in using a non-exec.
- A number of attempts have been made to define the elements of the role and contribution of non-execs, of which that by 3i is perhaps the most comprehensive and succinct, as well as being relevant to a wide range of types and sizes of organization.
- The public sector now also embraces many of the ideas which underpin the use of non-execs. Although some of the objectives and success criteria are different in the public sector, management effectiveness and corporate governance are increasingly seen as important issues which transcend questions of sector. Consequently, 'management' as a skill area has increased in importance and relevance even in those fields traditionally seen as the preserve of the technical specialist – e.g., the professions, the public services, and so on.
- Perhaps the key requirement of any non-exec is to add value to the organization of which he is part. With the increased ability and readiness to measure an individual's contribution and the extent to which he is in fact adding value, it is difficult for an under-performer to find a place to hide.

2
How SMEs Tick

Definition of SMEs

The principal thesis of this book is that SMEs are different, and their requirements in terms of non-executive directors are different from larger businesses. It would be as well to begin by defining what is meant by 'small-to-medium-sized' companies – for there is no textbook definition for a term of extremely wide currency. Interestingly, even the Federation of Small Businesses, in its capacity as the mouthpiece and advocate for the sector, does not place an upper limit on the size of businesses it claims to represent, instead leaving its largest category of member as '101-plus' employees.

The 1985 Companies Act attempted to define both 'small' and 'medium-sized' companies according to a set of criteria – sales turnover, balance sheet value, and number of employees. 'Small' companies were defined as satisfying any two of the following:

- sales turnover up to £1.4 million per annum;
- balance sheet value not more than £700,000;
- not more than 50 employees.

'Medium-sized' companies were defined in the Act as satisfying any two of the following:

- sales turnover up to £5.75 million per annum;
- balance sheet value not more than £2.8 million;
- not more than 250 employees.

It may be argued that the employee number criterion is still relatively valid, especially given what has happened to employment patterns over the past fifteen years and the extent to which various forms of automation have increased. It is suggested, however, that the two financial criteria must be viewed nowadays with a scepticism born of experience of the unprecedented escalation in corporate turnovers and profits seen in the wake of the liberalizing policies of the second and third Thatcher ministries.

Department of Trade statistics show small enterprises as making up a very significant proportion of businesses in Britain, accounting for almost one-half of all employment. Again, this statistic is not wholly qualified; what is, however, more precise is that 94 per cent of businesses in Britain employ 10 people or fewer, and 97 per cent employ 20 or fewer.[18] On reflection, this is perhaps not too surprising, since the 'businesses' referred to include shops and family concerns most of which employ only a couple of people at most and may, in many cases, technically have no 'employees' as such at all. Sales turnover is perhaps a more sensitive matter, for which information is not always quite so forthcoming, but given such figures as VAT and Corporation Tax thresholds it seems reasonable to assume that there are a vast number of businesses whose turnover is below £100,000 per annum. However, it may also be reasonable to assume that a substantial proportion of that 'vast number' do not seek, nor would they to any meaningful extent benefit from, the input of a professional non-executive director.

For the purposes of this work, the term 'small-to-medium enterprise' will cover businesses turning over *up to* somewhere in the region of £20 million per annum. It is impossible to be absolutely precise, for clearly there is no line which is indelibly drawn. The probability is that the majority of those companies which would see themselves, or be perceived by others, as being in the SME category turn over between £2 million and £10 million per year, whilst the tails of the bell-curve go down virtually to zero (representing new starts) and up to maybe £20 million to £30 million turnover, probably depending on the type of business. Some of these enterprises will be passing through the SME stage, as it were, on their way from start-up to being big, but the majority will be more or less permanently in the SME category. In most instances it is unlikely that such a distinction makes a major difference to the basic role of the non-exec, though occasionally it may do, as will be explained later. Significantly, however, we are talking about unlisted companies, to which Stock Exchange rules do not apply.

As for number of employees, this too depends (to a larger extent than turnover) on the type of business – a company could break through the £20 million barrier with perhaps a handful of employees or with perhaps tens or even hundreds. A suggested upper limit for the SME would be, say, about 200 employees, but in reality this is even more arbitrary than £20 million turnover and certainly no more precise.

Management characteristics

What may however be easier to define are some of the management characteristics. Most SMEs will tend to have owner–managers, perhaps because they are family companies where the equity is passed on from generation to generation, or perhaps because they have recently come into existence as start-ups or buy-outs/buy-ins. (For a more detailed consideration of the particular characteristics of family companies, see the last part of this chapter.) In some, all those managing the business will have a stake in the ownership, in others only certain among them: in most cases, the directors are likely to be significant shareholders, and this in itself can give rise to a problem. For under the law, directors' responsibility is to the shareholders, and it is the shareholders' advantage which they should continuously be seeking rather than their own; if, however, directors and shareholders are one and the same it can lead to a kind of *'l'état, c'est moi'* attitude in which nobody else's interests are given any consideration at all and the company becomes rather inward-looking, essentially a plaything of the directors rather than a serious endeavour to produce genuine added value on someone's behalf. This *may* (just!) be all right in a family concern or in a small private business, but it certainly won't work properly if there are any outside shareholders, particularly institutional ones, and it won't work if the company wants to become anything bigger and more significant. Smallness is in many respects as much an attitude of mind as anything else, to the extent that if you *think* like a small company you will only ever *be* a small company. It is all too easy for shareholder–directors to think in terms of a small company, and of their own interests as paramount, and such an attitude will almost certainly inhibit development.

A recent survey published in *Management Matters* (March 1999) listed what it said were the six commonest problems encountered by small businesses:[19]

- inadequate turnover volume;
- excessive government regulation and the associated paperwork;

- cashflow (manifested in slow-paying debtors, inadequate bank facilities, etc.);
- competition from bigger businesses in the same sector or market;
- the total tax burden (including National Insurance contributions);
- lack of business skills.

The article actually suggested that number six – the lack of business skills – was perhaps the key problem because if it were remedied then the others could more readily be coped with. Most of those who have had anything to do with management would probably entirely agree with that sentiment, but at the same time it's one of those things that is very easy to say, much less easy to make real! And nowhere, probably, is that more true than in the new start-up business.

Many new starts are essentially entrepreneurial in spirit, full of people with boundless enthusiasm and ability who direct those qualities at *doing* things as distinct from *managing* them. There is often little in the way of a formal structure – indeed there is not always any need for a formal structure, because everyone knows what they and all their colleagues are supposed to be doing, and in any case there usually isn't the money to spare to sustain an overhead in the form of a bureaucratic organization. The strength of this type of business usually lies in its energy, its go-getting approach, its 'can-do' mentality; its weakness, on the other hand, tends to lie in its almost complete lack of internal control. There is often an almost total dependency on relationships: one falling-out, and the whole enterprise may be put in jeopardy. Nobody properly understands either the principle or the practice of accountability, so there is no effective mechanism for anyone to account for what they do or to be judged on what they have or have not delivered. Communications are often not good, because they are not formalized – all the people are (or think they are) in such close and constant touch, frequently in the same room, that they don't see any requirement for a formalized approach to communicating. (The reality often is that they talk to one another but don't communicate!) In fact, in this kind of organization it isn't just communications that are not formalized; all too often, nothing at all is formalized, and even the simplest of procedures – never mind rules and regulations – are seen as just getting in the way.

In companies such as these, the contribution of a non-exec needs to be to provide a kind of underpinning, an element of stability, to try to ensure that it doesn't break too many rules. He should ensure as far as possible that legal requirements are met, though it may simply not be possible to ensure that every 'i' is dotted and every 't' crossed. He should also try to help to lay the foundations of systems, because if the company is successful and grows, it will at some stage need proper systems; and he must encourage those running the company to develop both themselves and their colleagues and subordinates, so that as the business grows then its people and systems grow with it and it doesn't outgrow its strength. At the same time, however, he needs to try to ensure a sufficiently light touch so that the energy which was referred to earlier is not stifled.

The evolution of a company

There is a strong argument for regarding a company as being akin to a living thing which is capable of organic activity involving, to a greater or lesser degree and in differing combinations and permutations, all of its constituent parts. As such, it may be seen to exhibit characteristics which change as the company itself develops, and which themselves help to define the company in terms of its development and the stage it has reached in that process. Indeed, it is possible to see this as analogous to certain stages in individual human development such as infancy, maturity, and so on; to do so can help to understand some of the needs and pressures a company faces. Table 2.1 is an attempt at representing this.

The characteristics exhibited by a company at the various stages of its development are in fact remarkably consistent, and can readily be divided into recognizable groupings. The categories which are identified below relate to *tangible* things such as aspects of organization structure and systems, and *intangible* things such as management style and what is termed 'emotional atmosphere' (by which is meant the prevailing mood within the organization, the attitudes people display towards their work, towards each other, and towards the general performance and progress of the organization).

Some of the characteristics of a company in its infancy have already been described above, and the chart tries to encapsulate these – the enthusiasm and energy, the intolerance of what may be seen as bureaucracy (but may in reality be a set of rules or guidelines to which adherence may be essential for survival . . .), the lack of clear structure and lines of accountability, the tendency to flit from one thing to another without any notion of a coherent plan, the tendency to make systems up as they go along, and so on. An infant is barely capable of independent survival, and so too a company at this stage is extremely vulnerable: many don't

Table 2.1   The ages of a company

	Emotional atmosphere	Management structure	Management style	Systems
Infancy	enthusiasm impatience	flat little definition	'can do' butterfly approach	intuitive no delegation
	energy	no clear reporting lines	very informal	
Childhood	curiosity	more definition	ring-fencing	external discipline
	self-centredness	points of reference	informal	
Adolescence	ambitiousness	unstable, prone to change	blame culture	state of flux
	desire to change the world	built around individuals	intolerance	can they cope?
Maturity	determination	stable	formal	stable & robust
	confidence	delegation & reporting	protocols	documented
	breadth of vision		training & development	
Old Age	cynicism opposition to change complacency	unresponsive doesn't reflect real world	over-formal ostrich tendency look to golden age	rigid can they cope?

ever make it beyond infancy, proving incapable of withstanding the pressures and forces that assail them and going under before they get the chance to progress to the next stage.

The next stage, 'childhood', is a particularly interesting one, because it is in fact possible for a company to stick there for its entire existence and not progress any further, whereas a company that doesn't progress beyond infancy will not generally survive. A company in the childhood stage will be beginning to look outward slightly, seeking the possibility of more exciting opportunities for the future, although it will tend to view those in terms of extensions to what it is doing at present rather than in a more strategic context of totally new activities and possible collaboration with third parties. The structure will begin to acquire some shape, with 'points of reference' emerging in the form of agreed areas of responsibility and, perhaps, some notion of relative seniorities. There probably isn't a great deal of 'corporateness' yet, with most people tending to carry out their own exclusive functions and not concerning themselves over-much with the greater good of the organization, but it can be quite a stimulating environment in which to work and it is one which tends to appeal to those who don't like too much formality. The vulnerability of a company at this stage often centres around its systems, because such systems as it has tend to arise from external pressures (the need to submit returns to the likes of the Inland Revenue, Customs and Excise, management accounts to the bank, and so on) rather than from a recognition within the company that systematization and profession-alism are actually necessary for effective performance. A great many small businesses remain at this stage of evolution, and certainly any company that does remain here will never become very large.

An 'adolescent' company exhibits many of the characteristics of an adolescent person. Its ideas are invariably right, even when they keep changing at frequent intervals, and it very readily sees itself as an exem-plar of some particular theory or management 'fad'. The big danger here is that the flavour of any particular month is usually related to the skills or priorities of certain key (and usually charismatic) individuals, around whom a structure is built: this is fine for as long as they are around and are performing, but if their star wanes or if they leave and go elsewhere then there can all too easily be something of a vacuum left behind them. Also, because there are usually some pretty strong ideas around, it is all too easy for a culture of intolerance and blame to arise, which can in fact stifle development of both people and systems.

This development is very important for an adolescent company, as things may be in something of a state of flux where systems and people are both having some difficulty in coping. For at a certain stage in a company's evolution (from experience, one would suggest at between £1 million and £2 million turnover and once there are more than about ten to fifteen people) the whole essence of a business has to change. Flying by the seat of the pants will no longer do: the whole thing must be more systematic. People need assistants or subordinates, so there needs to be a structure with lines of responsibility and clear account-ability, delegation, clarification of roles, perhaps new specialisms brought in, almost certainly greater financial skill to juggle debtors, creditors, and predatory bank managers – in short, the company needs *management*. This transformation marks the emergence from 'adolescence' into 'maturity' for the company, and any company seeking truly long-term growth and success must make the leap.

The 'mature' company sees things strategically, and breeds the confidence and determination in its people to reach the goals identified. Its people understand what is expected of them, and 'buy into' the shared targets – partly, this is a result of a stability in the organization structure, with responsibilities defined and agreed, and partly also it is a result of a degree of formality that is quite simply not usually found in less mature organizations. Now there is an obvious danger of passing from formality into bureaucracy, where structure and systems exist almost for their own sake rather than as means to an end: the best safeguard that a 'mature' organization can employ lies in the way it trains and develops its people so that they don't just accept and utilize systems, they positively develop and enhance those systems with the result that there is a robustness to them which helps them to cope with change and prevents them from getting bogged down.

The fortunate companies, those that are successful in the long term, reach maturity and stay there. There are some, however, that pass through to yet a further stage, when they run out of steam and their horizons start once again to close in on them. The prevailing mood is one of negativity, the structure actively impedes, rather than encourages, progress, and instead of being prepared to meet challenges people spend their time whingeing about things not being what they used to be, and of course blaming everything and everyone else – the government, the unions, the competition, the beastly foreigners, the weather, and so forth. It is sometimes possible for an elixir to appear, in the form of fresh management or a new owner, and for some kind of renaissance to take place, but otherwise this kind of company will just stagger on, gradually becoming less and less successful, until its owners or its creditors put it out of its misery. The staggering on can last for a great many years, perhaps giving rise to the belief that the company is not really on its last legs, but the journey leads only in one inexorable direction.

The world is full of companies, of vastly different sizes and types, at all of the above stages of their evolution, and there are of course successes and failures at all stages. The significance this has for the SME is that everything tends naturally to be near the surface – the fewer layers there are in a company, the less easy it is to hide anything! So the characteristics described and discussed above will tend to be very obvious ones, and it will be relatively easy to discern what stage a company has reached, whether it has the potential to progress beyond that particular stage, and if so what sort of help is going to be necessary for it to do so. Specifically, if as part of its evolution the SME is also expanding significantly, it is vital to recognize where it is on the evolutionary scale and hence the changes that will need to take place.

There is a belief that in circumstances such as these it is useful for a small company to have someone around who understands how big companies organize themselves, the point being that an ambitious small company needs to organize itself like a 'miniature big company'. There is almost certainly some merit in this idea, but as was hinted at in the introduction there may be dangers, especially in getting close to business angels (who, of course, have a financial agenda as well as a management one). The principal and most obvious danger is that the individual concerned may lack the sensitivity to recognize some of the essential differences highlighted here between big and small companies, as well as perhaps becoming frustrated by the inability of a small enterprise to achieve as much in organizational terms as its larger counterparts. Such a lack of sensitivity could possibly lead to inappropriate decision-taking, and a sense of frustration may easily lead to a fractured relationship and a consequent dysfunctionality.

In any event it is quite likely that a non-exec in such a situation (that is, a small company trying to grow) will have to take a lead in installing the appropriate structure and processes, or at the very least will have to apply a significant degree of effort to bring about the kind of culture which is going to be hospitable to them. Whether or not you actually take the initiative, your colleagues may well look to you for this lead, and if so it is not really a challenge that can be avoided. It requires quite a high profile and a willingness to get your hands dirty, and if that's not what you're into then quite simply you should read no further because you shouldn't be a non-executive director of a small business.

If, however, it is what you're into, then you must also be sensitive to the stage in its evolution the company has reached, and tailor your input to what is required – and bear in mind, of course, that 'what is required' will change over time. It is vital that a non-exec recognizes this, for his role and input must reflect the company's requirements which themselves will change according to its place on the evolutionary scale. As a generality, the further up towards 'maturity' the company is, the less hands-on the non-exec needs to be, but if a company falls prey to the problems of 'old age' he may once again need to raise his level of direct involvement.

An example of tailoring to changing requirements is the case of S. who was once appointed as a non-exec to the board of a small family-owned company shortly after the death of the father who had started it and built it up. He hadn't actually done the dynastic bit particularly well: he had been something of a despot and had not allowed his sons any responsibility whatsoever in how the business was run, or indeed given them any information about operations, finances, or anything, with the result that on his death they hadn't a clue what to do! So S.'s earliest efforts were directed at getting some very basic systems up and running for producing control information so that at least they had the where-withal for monitoring the company's operations and could see where money was being made and where it wasn't. S. had to teach them how to use the information so that a sensible decision-taking process could take root; then, once it was clear where the profit was coming from, the company needed restructuring to cut out the parts that didn't make money and build up the parts that did. It was necessary to put in place a structure of defined roles and responsibilities to make the structure work; after that, plans for expansion were laid. Everybody paused for breath, the sons started actually running the business, and S. simply chaired the board meetings.

What was most important throughout the period described in the above example was the perception of the owner–directors that there was in the background some sense of direction for the business and their perception that they could rely on their non-exec to maintain that sense of direction. It was not a matter of anything as hard and fast as a 'strategy', for at that particular stage in the company's development that would have been considered as being more relevant to a business school when what was really wanted was practical, hands-on advice. But there was a real need for some sense of continuity and coherence, some idea that all the various things that were happening were in fact part of a joined-up whole of some kind.

It is to say the least questionable whether a small business necessarily needs all the trappings of text-book strategic plans, but what it does need is an overall view of where it is trying to get to and how each thing that is done contributes towards that goal. It is often simply not realistic (and not fair, either) to expect this sort of overview from the executives, who are of necessity up to their ears in today's schedule, today's bills, and today's shortages, so they need to be confident that their non-exec has that overview and that he maintains and updates it.

The psychology of the small business

It is also important to be sensitive to what can best be described as 'the psychology of the small business'. It should be remembered that the owner–director (or, indeed, the plural of that) can lead a very lonely existence. He has most likely put his house and goodness knows what else on the line in order to obtain the funding for his business – indeed, his backside is probably so far out of the window that it's out of sight. The tyranny of the personal guarantee may well mean that he has far more to worry about than just the everyday ups and downs that virtually all businesses – of no matter what shape or size – experience. Granted, he may stand to gain handsomely if the business is a roaring success, but realistically there is a less-than-even chance of that actually happening – most small businesses will fail in their first year or two, and of those that do not fail, very few really make much serious money for their owners. In the meantime, he has a bank manager who typically (alas!) knows and understands little about business, full stop, let alone the peculiar circumstances of the small business. He may have a venture capital backer, whose interest goes little further ahead than the end of his nose. His accountant may advise him on providing various bits of information for the Inland Revenue, Customs and Excise, the Registrar of Companies, and so on, but probably not a lot beyond that. How many in the financial sector know what goes on in *real* companies, and more particularly how many of them know anything about small companies? Regrettably, the answer appears to be 'very few'.

If common sense ruled the world, all bankers and venture capitalists as part of their training would be made to spend at least a year seconded to a small company, working among its management, so that they might understand better how things work and hopefully might become more user-friendly. It is, admittedly, unrealistic and unfair to expect those people to be all things to all men, but the world of finance does seem to be particularly rarified when it comes to comparison with, and awareness of, the harsh day-to-day world of the small business. The emphasis on security in banking, and on rate of return in venture capital, is of course understandable – and indeed justifiable in terms of the kind of business they're in – but there is a clear dysfunction between it and the have-a-go attitude without which an SME is unlikely to go anywhere. Unless or until that sort of dysfunction can be overcome, and a common language and mutual understanding can be established, neither side will get the best out of the other. What is especially unfortunate and frustrating is that there are in fact some heroic individual bankers and venture capitalists who do understand, and do speak the language. Unfortunately however, they do seem to be in a minority, which is a pity.

It is, all in all, very likely that the owner–director may see his non-exec as the only friend he has, and he will look to him to provide the comfort, the reassurance, even just the knowledge of being there, that he can't get anywhere else. It's surprising just how close to panic many SME directors are for much of the time, and just how valuable a calm voice and a rational approach to risk assessment and decision-taking can be.

SMEs and their people can also tend to be somewhat isolationist – most probably because of the kind of pressures referred to above. This is often manifested in an apparent belief that there is no-one else, and no other organization, facing comparable circumstances and comparable problems. Those who have experience in a number of SMEs know that such a belief is mistaken, but the trick is in convincing executive colleagues of this. The more personal experience a non-exec can draw on, the more credible he is likely to be. There was a period of several years when the author was a non-executive director of two SMEs, both manufacturers, both of a similar size, in quite closely related although separate and distinct market sectors, and it was fascinating to watch the development of these companies proceeding almost in parallel one with another. It was possible to see the same sorts of opportunities arising, as well as the same sorts of problems cropping up – and it certainly seemed to be quite useful for the full-time directors of each company to be reassured that the other company did face similar opportunities and problems, as well as learning from things the other company had done in the face of such situations.

The ability to truly empathize, then, and in doing so to adapt, is perhaps the most important single quality a non-exec can bring to an SME. If all your previous experience has been in large organizations, and you are newly in post as a non-exec on an SME board, do not expect to find yourself in familiar territory. Do not expect them necessarily to talk the same language as you do. But look for the similarities, the consonances, for there are bound to be some somewhere, and keep learning from them once you find them. Remember, though, that you will need to be a quick learner, because until you can appreciate what is going on and how the company ticks, you will frankly not be of much use to them. It is in fact amazing how many quite unsuitable 'matches' are promoted between businesses and non-execs – by banks, by venture capitalists, by local enterprise organizations – because nobody has taken the trouble to define what kind of course it is and what kind of horse is required! Wasting a fee can be awfully easy, and there should not be any excuse for it.

The family business

It is clearly worth devoting some exclusive attention to the family business because of its unique characteristics. Family-owned businesses are said to account for about three-quarters of all UK companies – but this statistic needs a bit of a health warning. While we may instinctively think of a 'family business' in terms of a corner shop or a local plumber or joiner, the author has for example also dealt regularly with a company turning over in excess of £50 million which is owned by a family trust. It is even arguable that until recently the ownership of the Virgin group was such that it could be described as a 'family business'.

The two most common models of family business are, probably, those managed on a day-to-day basis by some or all the members of a family and those with the 'maiden aunt syndrome' – the shares are held by extremely detached (and quite probably old) family members who take no part in the running of the business and aren't at all interested so long as they receive their regular dividend cheque. Sometimes this latter category of company will have fixed itself up with a highly competent and professional management team and will in fact be extremely successful (as is the case with the family trust-owned company mentioned above). In such a case the separation between *management* of the company and *control* is simply a fact of life and is not in itself terribly important – no more important for example than in a big PLC where, instead of maiden aunts, there are pension funds and investment institutions.

Where, however, the business is managed by members of the family, it is more likely that there will be problems. Families tend to have rows, and they don't stop doing this just because they're in a boardroom rather than in a sitting room! Those who spend a number of years as a non-exec in a family-owned and family-managed company are likely to find that part of their function seems at times to be to hold people's jackets while they fight. Now there is nothing intrinsically wrong with a bit of tension within a company, especially if it can be turned to creative use, but there is a dividing line between tension and outright falling-out which most management teams preserve intact. In a family, however, people seem rather easily to forget how to behave maturely, and arguments get much more acrimonious and much more personal than is usual (or healthy) for a management team. Trying to lead, or guide, or even weld together a team in such circumstances is not an easy occupation and calls for some particular skills, of which many will be highlighted in Chapter 3 under 'self-managing competencies'.

It is made more difficult, of course, by the element of unpredictability often present in family relationships. Where there are three or more family members of the same board or management team, there is often a constantly-shifting pattern of alliances in which some members gang up on others, and you don't necessarily know from one meeting to the next, or even from one day to the next, who will be on whose side. Often it would be funny if it weren't so serious in its potential to harm the business. But then, if you as a non-exec try to intervene in some way, it's entirely possible that the family will suddenly put aside their differences and unite in their opposition to you. So you may have to tiptoe around many issues, and use a great deal of guile in achieving objectives which can be seen as relevant and desirable. Fortunately, what tends to happen in real life is that, within the family grouping, there will be one or more individual members who are pre-eminent and who assume a leadership role which is accepted by the others; what a non-exec needs to do is to discover fairly quickly where the power lies, how it is exercised, and how best to become an accepted part of the decision-making structure. Even having done that, however, it is necessary to tread carefully because blood is still likely to be a lot thicker than water and while it may be perfectly acceptable for one family member to criticize another it may be absolutely unacceptable for an outsider to do so. You may find that, even in a company which isn't actually a family-owned business but in which, say, a couple of members of the managing director's family are employed (most probably because they cost less than would have to be paid for an equivalent employee in the market place), you need to be somewhat careful what you say about those people and their performance.

What can you as a non-exec do if a family member is underperforming? The answer is that you have to do the same as you would in a similar situation in a non-family company, namely try to initiate a series of events which will either neutralize the underperformance or bring about an improvement, and you have to do this on the basis of provable facts that will stand up to scrutiny. But you also have to accept that there is perhaps a greater possibility of your failing to bring this about, if the family choose to close ranks and abandon rationality. The best advice is probably not to persist too long if this happens – unless you are sure of the person at the top backing you and carrying the day in the near future, you're better out of a situation which is probably going to end in tears. If the company cannot sustain a proper management set-up, its chances of success are limited, and if it fails then you too may be associated with that failure. Put simply, you cannot afford to place your personal reputation at risk in this way (and of course it is particularly unwise when you are not in a position to exercise any meaningful element of control over the situation). You would most probably be well advised to resign as a director, but make certain you set out clearly in writing your reasons for doing so – and make certain you keep a copy of your resignation letter.

The other major problem that may be encountered with family companies is related to succession. Such statistics as are available tend to show that fewer than one-third of family-owned businesses are passed on to a second generation of the family, and no more than 10–15 per cent make it through to a third generation[20]. This attrition rate is probably partly because succeeding generations cannot really be expected to have the same enthusiasm for a project as those who originated it, and it may also be due to a lack of training on the part of the would-be inheritors – why go to all the bother of training and so on if the whole thing is going to be handed to them on a plate anyway? Surely *they* are not to blame if everything goes wrong once they have inherited it? This kind of attitude can still be seen today in some family companies, though probably less so than in the past.

If you are a non-executive director of a company which is likely to be handed on in a dynastic fashion, you may in fact be in a unique position to influence things for the good. You can evaluate how competent the next generation is, and suggest ways in which the inheritance process may be improved by, for example, grooming the inheritors for the day when they take control, or perhaps helping to put in place a structure to support them in those aspects where they need supporting. In extreme circumstances, of course, you can advise against handing on the particular baton to the next generation, perhaps suggesting instead that the company looks outside the family for some or all of its new top management. If this is what you really believe, and it is for whatever reason not accepted by those currently in control, it too could become a matter for resignation.

For all its sometimes fraught characteristics, there is no doubt that the family company is often an interesting and rewarding environment in which to be involved. There may sometimes be found a degree and type of commitment that you simply don't meet elsewhere; and if you are to any extent a student of human nature it can be a fascinating experience. But be warned – the environment can be far from benign, and some of the skills you need are even more specialized, and even more vital, than those needed by SME non-execs in general.

Summary of key points

- 'Small' and 'medium-sized' companies are defined by statute in terms of their sales turnover, balance sheet value, and number of employees.
- 94 per cent of businesses in Britain employ fewer than 10 people, and 97 per cent employ fewer than 20.
- For the purposes of this study, SMEs are defined as being mainly in the £2 m–£10 m turnover range, and as having *up to* 200 employees. In addition, they will be unlisted businesses.
- But size is also a matter of attitude – if you think like a small company, you will only ever be a small company.
- Inadequacy of business skills may be the biggest single problem faced by SMEs, as other common problems (related for example to lack of turnover, poor cash flow, competition, and the burdens of taxation and government regulation) are exacerbated by such inadequacy.
- It is in the new start that the lack of business skills is particularly noticeable and harmful, and the right contribution by the right non-exec can be of immense significance in laying the foundations for future success.
- A company can go through a number of recognizable stages as it evolves. These may be described as infancy, childhood, adolescence, maturity, and old age; each stage is marked by a range of identifiable characteristics. It is perfectly possible for a company to remain at one stage and never progress to the next.
- An effective non-exec must recognize which stage his company is at, and tailor his input to what is required and appropriate to that stage; he must also recognize that 'what is required' may change over time.
- Although an SME may not possess – or even need – anything quite as sophisticated as a 'strategy' (the main requirement being for most of the time 'survival') the non-exec does need to be able to provide the more objective focus that the day-to-day executives do not have the time or perhaps the ability to input.
- It is also important to be aware of the peculiar pressures in SMEs and the effects these can have upon those who work in them. Directors of SMEs can find themselves needing friendship and reassurance as much as technical or managerial advice!
- The family business presents a particular set of characteristics and problems to a non-exec, especially if it is managed on a day-to-day basis by family members. Relationships among family members, and between family members and an 'outsider', can be very unpredictable.

Fortunately, however, there will often be one or more individuals within a family management group who possess the necessary ability and charisma to assume a leadership role – though care is still needed on the part of the non-exec since blood usually proves to be thicker than water.

- Family businesses can also cause a non-exec some problems when the issue of succession occurs. Only a small percentage of family-owned companies are successfully passed on to the succeeding generation, and a non-exec may have a crucial role to play in this process, in grooming the next generation, in ensuring that a suitably supportive infrastructure is in place to underpin the changeover – even perhaps in determining whether the process in fact takes place or whether the company looks instead for outside management to come in and take over the reins.

3
The 'Competency' Approach

'Competency' as distinct from 'competence' in performance

It is currently fashionable to examine individuals' performance in terms of 'competencies'. There is a great deal of value in such an approach, as it offers somewhat more scope than a rigid structure based simply on skills, but the expression 'competency' is relatively new and it is legitimate to be concerned about clarifying terminology. In particular, there is some risk of confusion between 'competency' and 'competence', and indeed some writers alternate between the two, which is not helpful. It is as well, therefore, to clarify what is to be understood by the terms and how they will be used in this work.

The traditional usage of the term 'competence' refers to a more or less quantifiable expression of a person's *capability* or *performance* in a particular area, covering a set of points on a scale which lie between 'incompetence' at one extreme and 'excellence' at the other. As such, it is a descriptive term. In contrast, the modern usage of the term 'competency' is more substantive and relates more to a *set of behaviours* or *elements of behaviour* on the part of an individual which are usually associated with a successful outcome. Thus within a particular *competency*, there is room for an individual to demonstrate a level of *competence*.

It is important to be clear about this because, quite apart from anything else, as far as capability or performance are concerned it is not just 'competence' that is required of non-execs, it is something much more exceptional. In this chapter therefore the concern will be specifically with 'competency' – or, more particularly, with 'competencies' – since we are not concerned here with an evaluation of the competence levels of any particular individuals but rather with skill areas and behaviour sets, and with how and where these may be required and applied.

How competencies are manifested

Not long ago, I took part in a study of non-executive directors and their links with high performance in the boardrooms of UK companies. The study defined competencies as being 'the underlying behaviours which enable people to shine in a particular role...the factors which distinguish 'the best from the rest'...the things that really make a difference'.[21] They are not the same as qualifications or experience, nor are they in fact akin to skills or to levels of technical knowledge: indeed, they appear to be almost innate rather than acquired.

The study included experienced non-executive directors from a variety of backgrounds, and looked at their operations in organizations of a variety of types in both private and public sectors. It set out to identify a number of competencies that appeared to be common among successful non-executive directors, or at any rate among those who were *perceived* as being successful and as such might be characterized as being superior, as distinct from average, performers.

Because they relate to characteristic behaviours, competencies provide a useful model for developing a framework within which detailed descriptions may be made of how individuals perform and how they may be expected to perform. This in turn could be a valuable element in the process of selecting individuals for posts (many job specifications now actually spell out, at the recruitment/selection stage, competencies which will be required on the part of job holders) and of developing them throughout their career.

Competencies can offer clues to individuals' strengths and weaknesses and hence to their development needs, but also to their personal priorities, the things they feel to be important to them – in other words, what makes them tick. They can thus become a kind of 'overlap' between the zones covered respectively by ability testing and psychometric testing, and give major clues to the leadership and management styles which individuals are likely to adopt and the way in which those individuals may relate to the various *processes* of leadership and management.

Competency 'clusters'

In the study mentioned above, a total of 25 distinct competencies were identified and described in some detail. The identification arose out of

Table 3.1   Clusters of Competencies

Thinking	Getting Results
The range of competencies required to think through situations in different ways and from various perspectives to formulate ideas and generate vision	The range of competencies that may be required to ensure the delivery of outcomes, to the standards required by the business
Influencing	**Self Managing**
The range of competencies that may be required to ensure effective interaction with individuals and groups of people to gain the commitment of others	The range of competencies required to ensure effective self management within the demanding context of organisational life

highly structured narrative descriptions by the study participants – all experienced independent/non-executive directors – of situations and behaviours from their personal experience; the actual labelling was done by the researchers themselves on the basis of those descriptions. Once the competencies had been identified and described, they were grouped (again, by the researchers) into four 'clusters' each of which was defined in behavioural terms as representing a key area in the way in which people perform at work.

In a different 'cut', two distinct categories of competency were identified: distinguishing competencies, so named because the frequency with which examples were cited by the study participants indicated that these competencies were crucial to distinguishing 'the best from the rest'; and threshold competencies, which were clearly felt each to be important enough to form part of some kind of entry criterion for effective non-executive director performance, but not necessarily each to be crucial by itself.

Outside of these two defined categories, the researchers were able to identify other competencies whose frequency of mention suggested a pretty high level of significance, albeit less absolutely crucial than that of the distinguishing competencies. No particular adjective was applied to these – it was felt by the researchers that their significance might be specific to certain situations, in which case it would not be realistic to imbue them with the kind of universality that was implied in the labels 'distinguishing' or 'threshold'.

The competencies were grouped by the researchers into the four 'clusters' as already mentioned, on the basis that each cluster represented a major area in which a non-exec might be expected to make a significant contribution to an organization. The clusters formed a framework for analysis as shown in Table 3.1.

It is worth looking more closely at these, for they may well lead us in a useful direction in terms of identifying links between what a non-exec should *be* and what a non-exec should *do*.

Thinking competencies

In this cluster there were four distinct competencies identified:

- *Analytical thinking*, which involves breaking down problems and situations logically into their component parts, and using this breakdown as a framework for a diagnostic process and for developing solutions;
- *Forward thinking*, where an individual looks ahead and is able to anticipate the outcome (or, indeed, the several alternative outcomes) of a particular situation or course of action;
- *Conceptual thinking*, where an individual can understand 'the wider picture' – this not only covers the context in which something is occurring, but also encompasses an ability to discern patterns and connections between things which might seem on the face of it not to be related (sometimes known as 'lateral' thinking);
- *Strategic thinking*, which involves conceiving a vision for the future and translating this into a long-term plan for the development of the business.

All four of the above competencies may be said to represent an ability, or a range of abilities, in intellectual terms. Now it may be argued that a substantial intellect is actually a *sine qua non* of being a successful non-executive director, and of course the identification of the 'thinking' competencies would appear to bear out that view. It is interesting to note, however, that the study results suggested that those 'thinking' competencies were regarded by the majority of participants as being threshold but not distinguishing competencies. It is important to get this into perspective: *all* the competencies identified in the study were seen as necessary elements in the make-up of a successful non-executive director, so to categorize some as threshold rather than distinguishing is not an indication of a lesser *status* so much as of a different *relevance*. It is always possible that the study participants took the 'thinking' competencies for granted: what is perhaps more likely is that they attached more importance to action than to thought!

Getting results competencies

This was the biggest 'cluster', containing eight competencies:

- *Initiative*, describing those who seize an opportunity to take action *before* needing to be asked to do so;
- *Results focus*, where an individual is not satisfied unless a clear and definable – and indeed successful – outcome is achieved, and devotes substantial and consistent energy to this goal;
- *Thoroughness*, where an individual is concerned throughout a task or a programme of work to monitor and maintain standards of accuracy and completeness on a continual basis, and to ensure that the required levels of detail are sustained;
- *Determination*, where an individual devotes sustained or repeated effort towards the goal, often over a long period of time, often overcoming several obstacles which may or may not have been foreseen;
- *Critical information seeking*, which involves an active seeking after information combined with a process of distinguishing what is relevant and weeding out what is not, and a systematic building up of an information base relevant to the successful achievement of the business' goals and objectives;
- *Concern for standards*, which is characterized by an ongoing and relentless drive for excellence – of product, service and relations with stakeholders;
- *Concern for efficiency*, where an individual is constantly looking for and driving through improvements or searching for new ways of doing things;
- *Developing people*, which is manifested in a genuine desire to foster learning and development in others in the organization, not for motives of altruistic benevolence but because the individual recognizes that improving the performance of a business's people will improve the performance of that business.

These all suggest a role which is essentially pro-active. Indeed, the first and possibly most pro-active of the above competencies, 'initiative', was the only one in this cluster identified as a distinguishing competency. This is interesting, for it tends to add some weight to the ideas about 'independence' discussed earlier. Clearly, those who took part in the research had no intention of being 'nodding donkeys' or other passive types, and saw no value in having those types among their number. 'Critical information seeking' and 'thoroughness' were identified as threshold competencies: neither of these is at all surprising in the context of what must be essential elements in a non-exec's make-up, and indeed it is difficult to imagine any organization wanting to take on a non-exec who didn't display them.

Influencing competencies

This was the second largest cluster, in which the researchers identified a total of seven competencies:

- *Interpersonal awareness*, meaning that the individual not only is aware of, but also makes every effort to understand, the needs, concerns and interests of others;
- *Concern for impact*, which covers a high level of sensitivity to the impact the individual has on others in terms of his manner, bearing, tone, words, actions, and so on. The individual anticipates others' needs and tries to respond to those by using appropriate words, actions, and so forth so as to achieve a successful outcome;
- *Persuasiveness*, meaning the ability to construct compelling arguments based on objective elements such as logic and a lucid analysis of facts;
- *Organizational awareness*, by which is meant that the individual understands how an organization hangs together and functions – how, for example, different groups within an organization link up, how these links change and form patterns, and how working practices are based on such links and the interdependencies they foster;
- *Strategic influencing*, where an individual understands the reasons for, sources and types of, influence with other individuals and groups within the organization, and gives conscious consideration to choosing the most suitable sources and types of influences in order to achieve a specific goal or outcome;
- *Relationship building*, where an individual creates and nurtures a network of contacts both within and outside the organization with an eye to the long-term benefits which the organization may derive from this;
- *Situational sensitivity*, which covers the intelligent use of the individual's 'antennae' to determine the essentials of different situations in terms of their impact on people, and the ability (and willingness) to modify behaviour in the light of situations and impacts.

All the above clearly relate to how one fits into one's context, in terms of relationships, interactions, and so on, and highlight the significance of achieving results through other people. This may be of particular importance for non-executive directors, whose position largely precludes them from achieving results directly themselves and whose impact therefore may depend to a great extent on what they can achieve through others and how they can succeed in doing so. From this list, 'strategic influencing' was identified by the participants as the sole distinguishing competency, while 'concern for impact', 'organisational awareness', and 'situational sensitivity' were the threshold competencies. It is interesting to note how much significance the participants attached to the effectiveness of a non-exec's 'antennae' and how those antennae served to influence his actions.

Self-managing competencies

Six competencies were identified under this heading:

- *Self-control*, demonstrated by those who continue to perform effectively under conditions of stress and difficulty, largely by keeping their emotions under control;
- *Independence*, which in this context means being able and willing to raise issues of importance in situations when to do so courts actual or potential opposition;
- *Self-development*, meaning that an individual takes continuous action to develop and enhance his own personal capability;
- *Positive self-image*, which allows an individual to maintain and project a high degree of self confidence as a result of a belief in his own ability;
- *Flexibility*, meaning the willingness of an individual to adapt the approach taken to a situation so as to suit the particular needs or circumstances of such a situation;
- *Organizational commitment*, meaning the ability and willingness of an individual to align his own behaviour with the objectives and values of the organization.

This cluster is all about how the individual stands and operates *as an individual*, without a team or a superior or a mentor. It contained the largest number of identified distinguishing competencies, with three – 'self-development', 'positive self-image', and 'flexibility' – being so identified; interestingly, *all* the participants in the study identified themselves as possessing the first and second of those! 'Independence' was, not surprisingly, seen as a threshold competency.

The picture formed by distinguishing competencies

So the study participants identified five distinguishing competencies out of a total of twenty-five: initiative, strategic influencing, self-development, positive self-image and flexibility. That is fairly selective, plumping only for one in five, and suggests in itself something about the discriminating powers of those who operate as non-execs. Presumably those individuals who took part in the study were being honest in describing what they had said, thought, and done in the case studies they offered, so it seems therefore to be the considered opinion of a fairly representative group of non-execs that possession of those five is a necessary precondition to effectiveness in a non-executive role. That opinion is all the stronger for having arisen from a research process which was designed in such a way as to maximize the objectivity of the results.[22] So is that what a non-exec sees when he looks in the mirror? or when he looks around himself at gatherings of non-execs and tries to identify the best of them?

The answer is very probably 'yes'. For while many non-execs may possess – or may like to think they possess – other attributes, it is true to say that without those five competencies they might be highly effective in certain areas but not as non-execs. Let us examine why.

Firstly, *initiative*. The study summed this up as taking action before needing to be asked to do so. It is an element of leadership, but it is also what you might call a 'moving and shaking' element – people who show initiative help to shape events, rather than respond to them. They may not invariably be successful, and it may be that sometimes when they *are* successful there is a measure of luck in that, but it seems fairly obvious that there is a degree to which one can help to make one's own luck, and it is people with initiative who do this. (There is also a point to be made here, in passing, that you can be 'lucky' without actually making anything of it – but people with initiative do tend to ride their luck and put it to some positive use.) Many of the items that were considered previously – such as assuming the duty of care, satisfying oneself that one is properly informed, maintaining one's independence, adding value, and so on – require a high degree of initiative in the sense that waiting for someone else to make the first move is not a realistic option. The making of that first move doesn't necessarily have to consist of taking some dramatic action; it might be simply offering an opinion, finding out the answer to a bothersome question, setting up a contact or a helpful meeting with a third party – whatever, it is a case of being 'on the front foot' and adding the value without it having to be sought. Put crudely, you are on the board as a non-exec because of what you can bring to the party, and it's a pretty odd party and you're a pretty odd invitee if you have to be *asked* to hand over what you've brought.

Secondly, *strategic influencing*. This was described by the researchers in terms of understanding how patterns of influence work in an organization, and using such understanding in order to achieve a specific goal or outcome. To do this might seem to imply a degree of manipulativeness on the part of the non-exec, and indeed that is probably a fair comment – it goes with the 'initiative' mentioned above, and points to a pro-active approach to the job. Now, what is meant by 'manipulativeness' here is not deviousness, so much as an ability to put yourself in others' shoes and try to behave as you might if you were they. The non-exec needs to have regard to the long term, even if necessity demands that he get involved at times in essentially short-term matters, and it is in part the degree of influence which he exerts over the long term that determines his success or otherwise. By understanding how and why others behave, and by discerning the 'patterns of influence', he puts himself in a position to exert such influence. In reality this may be more relevant in larger organizations than in small, since in the latter type there are not really likely to be as many cliques or 'political' groupings, but even in a small company with, say, only a couple of executive directors, it may be a significant element in the non-executive contribution.

If there is a powerful outside interested body, such as a venture capital investor, the issue of 'patterns of influence' can be very important. It makes sense, when being appointed to a board in the position of institutional nominee, to try at an early stage to establish exactly how far the institution wants to be involved with management decision-taking, for sometimes the institution has a very definite agenda and you need to have regard to that as their nominee or else your relationship with them will sooner or later (probably sooner!) become dysfunctional.

This may in fact be easier said than done – an institution may be surprisingly reticent, coy even, about its agenda, and you may have difficulty in reading the tea leaves. A non-exec once came badly unstuck in the course of one particular directorship when the investor institution which had nominated him appeared to change its agenda (without actually having briefed him about the change) and he found himself in effect acting against it rather than on its behalf. Unfortunately the situation was one in which he needed its support for a course of action he was initiating, and at the crucial point in time that very support was not forthcoming. The upshot was that he lost his directorship, and the institution lost its credibility with the executive directors. The charge against him, probably, is that he did not cotton on soon enough to a shift in the patterns of influence, and thus was unable to achieve the specific goal or outcome he sought because he backed the wrong side.

Thirdly, *self-development*. Once again, this is linked to initiative. What it means in practical terms is that because you as a non-exec are likely to be around on only a part-time basis, the onus is on you to maintain your usefulness and relevance and to keep pace with the development of the organization. Today's people can soon become yesterday's people, and yesterday's people will astonishingly quickly become last week's people, so if you're to add value and go on adding it you must make sure you develop your knowledge and understanding of the organization and grow with it. As has been pointed out already, there is no guarantee that a non-exec will find himself appointed to a company of a type, or in a sector, with which he is previously familiar, so there is a task to be accomplished in getting up to speed as rapidly as possible – and in keeping up, once there.

The executives in a company may well devote some effort to their own personal development and training (although regrettably it has to be said that this is an area that is neglected in many SMEs), but you can't reasonably expect them to do the same for you as their non-exec. So it's up to you. Up to a point, you may find the exercise of self-awareness and reflection useful, but there are limitations in terms of just how objective you can be, particularly if your situation is one involving a significant degree of stress. Up to a point, you may be able to seek some kind of feedback from your executive colleagues, though that is likely to depend very much on the sort of relationship you have with them, and as already discussed *that* may not be altogether within your control. Occasionally one may be able to obtain such feedback on a one-to-one basis from an individual executive, and in one instance involving the author it turned out to be of key importance because it exposed a perception within the board that he was perhaps 'ducking' a particular issue at that time, and as a result he was able to sharpen his focus and tackle the issue in question, with ultimately successful results.

Membership of professional bodies such as the Institute of Directors can be most valuable here: they run courses and seminars, they publish booklets and papers, and they facilitate access to the sorts of networks by means of which it is possible to keep up-to-date with managerial thinking and also with developments in various business sectors. On a similar tack, there are often local 'networks' at whose meetings one tends to bump into lots of other people who are doing the same kind of work, and it is often both interesting and instructive to 'swap notes' about situations and compare how different people have tackled similar problems. At gatherings like these, it is impossible *not* to be struck by the extent to which individuals have sought answers to situations by developing their own expertise rather than relying on someone else to come up with a solution.

Turning fourthly to the matter of *positive self-image*, it would be easy to say this is a polite term for arrogance! Reading any literature about non-executive directors, one is conscious of a strong element of self-assurance which seems to underpin much of what they are about. The same kind of impression also comes across whenever several non-execs are gathered together: they tend to use their own points of reference when analysing or evaluating situations, rather than relying on external or 'established' points of reference.

In essence, it's not all that different from the *esprit de corps* that may be found for example among management consultants or, indeed, any professional group with a strong and cohesive identity. It is partly a recognition that you're all under pressure, you're all facing situations of a kind that most of your peers have faced and have dealt with successfully, and the principal reason you're all where you are is that someone reckons you have the ability to succeed. But that, perhaps, is a crucial part of the key here – internally, there may be an expectation of success, but this must be externalized, and if you are touting yourself as the answer to an organization's need, you have to work at selling yourself, convincing them that you are a 'must have'. For this to be truly effective, you surely have to believe it yourself, otherwise it is difficult to see how you can realistically expect others to believe it of you.

But there is still more to it than that. Reference has been made in earlier chapters to the issue of matching horses to courses: it is fairly obvious that at some point a non-exec is going to find himself in unfamiliar territory in terms of the type of organization, or business sector, he goes into, and in all probability he is going to have to rely largely on his own wit and ability to survive initially and to become a value-adder thereafter. Like it or not, part of this is going to be down to the perception held of him by the management of the client organization (who may, remember, be somewhat suspicious at first – after all, who the hell is this outsider, possibly imposed on them by their institutional investor, who is going to come in and monitor, and perhaps pontificate on, the way the business is run?) and that perception can be influenced in a major way by the non-exec's bearing and behaviour. So if in fact you're treading water for a while, it is obviously very important not to let them know that you are. Appear confident and in control, and by and large people will believe that you are: appear hesitant or unsure of yourself, and people will wonder what they are paying for!

From the other end of the pipe, there is at times something of a perception among organizations that non-execs are a breed apart. They represent an additional cost, they bring (or claim to bring) a different perspective, perhaps they even play to a slightly different script – they are *in* the organization but not *of* it. In such circumstances, it would be surprising if non-execs did not gain a positive feeling of being slightly special.

But at the end of the day, a non-exec may have to shoulder a pretty sizeable responsibility. Not only in a Cadbury-related situation, but also at times of commercial or financial stress, it may be up to the non-exec/s to determine the fate of other directors or even of the company itself. That is an exposed position to be in, irrespective of the size of business, and to cope effectively with it a fair degree of self-belief is necessary and indeed desirable. Thinking about actions you have taken or might be about to take against other individuals can be a recipe for sleepless nights: several of the case studies which form Part II of this book illustrate situations in which such actions have become necessary, and there must be relatively few sentient beings who could live with having gone out on a limb somehow, or having done something unpleasant, unless they are truly confident that it was the right thing. Nor, indeed, could most people contemplate with equanimity going into a situation they knew to be actually or potentially problematic unless they had a high degree of confidence in their own ability to manage that situation and emerge on the far side with a degree of success.

Fifthly and finally, let us look at *flexibility*. This may need a health warning: it can be both an enviable and a dodgy attribute. Someone can rightly be praised for being adaptable, not set in their ways, quick on their feet, able to change focus if circumstances demand – all those things which can be seen as setting survivors apart from dinosaurs. But flexibility might equally mean a certain shiftiness, a lack of a stable and coherent value system, a tendency to bend with the wind – not, perhaps, altogether what those who appoint non-execs are looking for. (However, it is worth noting that oak and bamboo are both valuable and valued species, though each in their different ways, and in the different contexts in which their particular attributes are of relevance.)

In the context of the competency study, flexibility was defined in terms of an individual's ability to adapt to changing circumstances and to suit one's approach and input to the particular situation in which one found oneself. This must make sense – especially in small businesses, where quickness-on-the-feet is often part of what separates the successful from the rest, and this is a good example of why there is a question mark about the suitability as SME non-execs of those whose experience has all been in large organizations. The decision-making process in an SME will, almost by definition, nearly always be faster and less bureaucratic than that in a large company, and because of that an SME is often able to change course more readily in response to changes in, for example, customer preferences, market conditions, supply costs, and so on. It shouldn't necessarily be seen as a sign of weakness or top-level indecisiveness for an organization to act flexibly in this way; indeed, it is not difficult to envisage situations where it is an absolute necessity because the organization doesn't have the 'fat' to live off during what could, if allowed, be an extended period of coming to terms with some crucial external change. A large organization is more likely to have such 'fat' and therefore can afford for its change of course to be more gradual, planned and systematic. It is, if you like, part of an organization's culture, and it is important that a non-exec is in tune with that culture if he is to make any worthwhile contribution.

The point was also made earlier about small companies living life nearer the edge than larger ones. This too demands a degree of flexibility simply in order to survive! The margin for error is narrower, while the penalty for getting it wrong is more immediate and most probably more terminal. There really is not much of a place in an SME for the hidebound or the unimaginative – quite the reverse, in fact, for what is truly valuable is surely a degree of creativity not always associated with 'management' as taught and practised. It is easy to find oneself in a situation which seems similar in some respects to situations one has been in before, but to sense that what 'worked' before isn't going to 'work' this time. What is taught at business school *can* be extremely valuable, but most especially if it is viewed as guidance rather than being treated as formulaic.

However, there remains the question of constancy of values. This is in fact an important issue (see for example the earlier reference to PRO NED's emphasis on 'matters of principle rather than of practice'). Although it didn't crop up specifically in the competency study, there is undoubtedly a strong argument that people's values will be reflected in their competencies. Moreover, there does seem to be a general recognition, particularly post-Cadbury, of an ethical dimension to conducting business, to which it is almost axiomatic that non-execs should make a major contribution. On one level, it is suggested several times in this work that a non-exec may be looked to by colleagues as an exemplar of good practice; on another level, the kinds of issues with which non-execs become concerned are (when their hands are not getting dirty) those relating to how the business is run, how its employees, customers, and creditors are treated, and how generally the organization behaves.

Because the non-exec is so often in a position of being expected to give advice, guidance, counsel, and so on, it is surely preferable that those seeking such things can expect them to be rooted in a coherent and recognizable value system. Flexibility of approach does not in any way have to undermine a value system, or vice-versa – indeed, the one can often strengthen the other by demonstrating awareness of limits, for unlimited flexibility is probably a recipe for chaos and ultimate self-destruction, while unlimited or uncompromising adherence to a system of values or beliefs has throughout history rarely brought with it anything other than grief on one scale or another.

Distinguishing competencies and SMEs

So it really can be demonstrated that the five distinguishing competencies are crucial to effectiveness as a non-executive director. However, the study did not in fact differentiate by size or type of organization: most of the participating directors sat on both SME and PLC boards, with only three or four individuals relating *only* to SMEs. To some extent, therefore, the question must arise as to how far the picture is specifically relevant to SMEs as such.

It has been suggested that in certain instances – for example, when considering self development and flexibility – there is a particular relevance to the SME. In the case of self development, it is linked to the likelihood that training and development of any sort will be a relatively neglected area, primarily for simple reasons of resource availability (or lack of it); while in the case of flexibility it is really at the heart of what characterizes a small business.

But there has to be more to it than that. As previously noted, only five of the competencies out of a total of twenty-five were identified as distinguishing competencies. Does such a high degree of selectivity apply across all types and sizes of organizations, or can some differentiation be identified by size or type? In particular, is the distinction claimed by the survey's authors between threshold and distinguishing competencies in fact a valid one to draw in the context of SMEs?

The key to this may lie in the statement about 'distinguishing the best from the rest'. The smaller the organization, the less room there will be for anyone not pulling their full weight, and it must be crucially important that a non-exec in an SME isn't there just to make up the numbers or to satisfy the terms of the shareholders' agreement or the articles of association. The insistence on the need to add value, posited at the end of Chapter 1, is based on a real concern for the impact (positive or negative) a non-exec can have on an SME. Moreover, the sheer breadth and variety of roles and circumstances encountered by the SME non-exec could be said to underline in the strongest possible way a need to have 'the best' rather than 'the rest'.

So if indeed distinguishing competencies really are the touchstone for exceptional performance by a non-exec, then surely it is realistic to claim that they have supreme relevance to SMEs. But by itself, the 'competency' framework for identifying and evaluating non-execs' performance has limitations. Specifically, what it doesn't do is examine how a number of competencies may actually group together to deliver an identifiable role, and although it would arguably be wrong to treat competencies and roles as an 'either/or' choice, it is specifically in the examination of roles that we really come to the heart of what an SME non-exec is, does, and is worth.

Summary of key points

- 'Competencies' are much in vogue nowadays as a means of defining both the requirements for a job and the extent to which it is being satisfactorily performed. In such a context, a 'competency' means a skill area and set of behaviours usually associated wiith a successful outcome.
- A study in 1998 of successful non-executive directors identified a number of competencies which appeared to be shared by all participants. A total of 25 distinct competencies were identified and described in some detail, and out of these certain were characterized as 'distinguishing' competencies (seen as being absolutely crucial to separating the best from the rest) and certain others as 'threshold' competencies (seen as forming a kind of entry criterion for effective non-exec performance).
- The 25 competencies were grouped into four 'clusters' – thinking, getting results, influencing, and self-managing competencies. No distinguishing competencies were identified in the thinking cluster; in the other clusters a total of five were identified. These were initiative

(from the getting results cluster), strategic influencing (from the influencing cluster), and self-development, positive self-image, and flexibility (from the self-managing cluster).

- Detailed consideration of the five distinguishing competencies, and relating them to personal experience, tends to support their selection. While non-execs may often possess other valuable attributes, without the distinguishing competencies they would not be likely to achieve optimum effectiveness in their role.

- In a small organization there is no room for anyone who does not pull his full weight, hence it is vitally important for a non-exec to add real value. This, coupled with the range and variety of roles and circumstances he may need to deal with, emphasizes the need for SMEs to have 'the best' rather than 'the rest'.

- However, a set of competencies by themselves will not necessarily fully define a role within an organization, and it is in examining roles that the real heart of the non-exec issue is reached.

4
Is There a Universal SME Non-Exec?

In conceptual terms, it seems fairly clear that high performance on the part of a non-executive director is going to depend on the congruence of four key factors:

- the individual's knowledge
- his skills
- the experience he brings to bear and
- his competencies.

The way these interact and overlap may be illustrated diagrammatically, as shown below.

However, it is all very well drawing meaningful-looking diagrams and dealing in concepts: when you are at the board table things are 'for real' and concepts are not a great deal of use unless you can translate them into practical actions, real behaviour patterns and genuine roles.

The 'Competency' approach discussed in the previous chapter led in the direction of identifying a kind of paradigm – not exactly an 'identikit' SME non-exec, for that would tend to imply that you could almost construct your own to order, and that hardly does justice to the skills and qualities required in non-execs. But it is, nevertheless, legitimate to examine whether there is an ideal, or universal, model which could be created conceptually and then used as a standard against which to judge individuals. What follows therefore is an attempt to define, within some kind of structure, the different roles it is suggested the SME non-exec has to adopt from time to time, based as far as possible on empirical evidence from real-life experiences and encounters. If the presumptions are right, then these roles should in sum draw together the strands set out in Chapters 1 to 3 into a coherent whole.

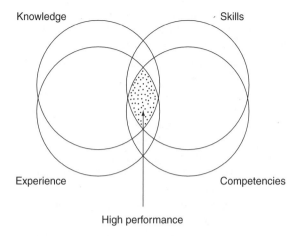

Knowledge · Skills

Experience · Competencies

High performance

Figure 4.1 Congruence of factors leading to high performance

The leader

Throughout this book so far there has been a degree of emphasis upon the need for a non-exec in an SME to be prepared to take the initiative and, if necessary, get his hands dirty. Now clearly this is not just something you do for the fun of it. There has to be a reason for getting your hands dirty, and that reason has to be aimed in the general direction of the issue of necessity for the survival or success of the enterprise, and the need for someone to take on a leadership role. There is at least anecdotal evidence to suggest that this occurs quite frequently, and it is often argued that the ability and willingness to have dirty hands is an essential part of leadership – you will not invariably be successful as a leader by cultivating a 'distance' between yourself and those you lead.

Leadership is a vast area of study in itself, and no doubt this entire book could have been devoted to it – though it certainly would not have been the first to do so. It happens to be one of the easiest aspects of management to get wrong, and it is entirely possible that in fact the extent of that wrongness is a major cause of failure and inefficiency in business.

Perhaps the principal way in which so many people get it wrong is to confuse *leadership* with *management*. Bennis's well-known saying 'Managers do things right: leaders do the right thing'[23] highlights where the difference lies – leadership is far more about setting the agenda, establishing goals and standards, mapping something out, whereas management is about delivering the agenda, fleshing out and realizing goals and using maps to assist in reaching objectives. So good managers will not necessarily make good leaders (and of course the converse is no less true). This may become a problem in, for example, new start-ups and some management buy-outs, where individuals who had not previously been leaders are suddenly required to don such a mantle.

It ought to be possible to summarize what leadership is, in order that we may assess its significance in the context of a non-exec's role. Various authorities have tried to do this, particularly since the period between the two world wars which could be said to have marked the start of the systematic study of management. Even more particularly, the period since the end of World War II, with its relative economic stability and increasingly internationally-minded business community, has seen many attempts on both an academic and a practical plane to identify what it is that successful organizations do, in order that others may do likewise, and the extent to which this may be predicated on the substance and style of a leader. What is most noteworthy, however, is the fact that nobody has yet actually found the philosopher's stone! Examples of individuals and organizations cited as outstandingly successful, and urged on the rest of us as role-models, all too frequently turn out later not to have been quite so successful as had once seemed the case. Fads and fashions, unfortunately, appear to play almost as big a part as rational argument in defining what is or is not good practice. Leadership has not been immune to this; it is perhaps not too difficult to define what its substance is (one of the best such definitions being that of Kotter, writing in 1990,[24] who distilled it into three key tasks: establishing a direction of travel, aligning people so that they buy into that direction, and motivating and inspiring them by appealing to a combination of their needs, values, and emotions) but extremely difficult to define how best it should be practised. Authoritarian, exploitative, participative, action-centred – all these styles and others have had their proponents and, indeed, exponents, variously claiming success.

However, arguably one of the most persuasive approaches to the issue of leadership style is that encapsulated in the concept of 'situational leadership', as developed in the 1960s by management scientists, notably Hersey and Blanchard.[25] Their argument is, briefly, that there is not necessarily a *universally* 'right' style of leadership but that the most appropriate style will vary according to the circumstances the enterprise finds itself in. During the 1960s there was a vogue for what might be

called 'liberal' management styles, where hierarchies were less important than communicating relationships, and a democratic, rather than
autocratic, approach was touted as best practice. It was pointed out
that, in the past, the only reason people had tended to come together in
organized groups was to make war or to defend themselves against
someone else who was making war on them; in such circumstances,
hierarchies and chains of command were vitally necessary, and more or
less unthinking obedience to orders was more likely to be a recipe for
survival than was a readiness to engage in discussion and debate as to
the relative merits of alternative courses of action! In business, so the
argument went, this wasn't relevant or indeed desirable: people would
perform much better if given a freer rein and an element of freedom to
take initiatives for themselves. Moreover, there was undoubtedly
a strong argument to the effect that as people became better and better
educated, unquestioning obedience was less and less of an acceptable
option, and discussion and debate would become more the norm.

This was fine, up to a point, that point being the dividing line
between success and problems, or between stability and difficulty. It began
to be realized that, in business, the going could indeed get tough, and
that when it did get tough there was a greater need for action and
a reduced scope for free reins. Hersey and Blanchard systematized this
realization into a theory which allowed for an easy-going hands-off
style of leadership when everything was going smoothly but which
recognized that when an organization hit problems it was quite legitimate – indeed, appropriate and necessary – to ditch democracy and adopt a
more autocratic approach. The trick, of course, for an effective leader
was having the intelligence and sensitivity to recognize how benign or
hostile the operating environment was, and to be able to adjust his style
accordingly.

For leadership to be effective, after all, there must also be present an
element of what may be called 'followership' – unless people are prepared
to follow you (however gladly or sullenly) you cannot really claim to be
a leader. I encountered a vivid illustration of this early on in my career,
working in a large group for H., a divisional MD within the group.
Although not an overtly charismatic individual, H. was without doubt
an outstanding 'leader'. He didn't pretend to have all the answers all the
time, but everybody round him felt that they had a part to play in his
decision-making processes and that their views and interests would be
fully considered, even if the eventual outcome wasn't exactly what they
might have wanted. He was quite capable of (usually metaphorically,
rather than literally) thumping the table and laying down the law if

that was what was needed, but he got what he wanted for the most part without resorting to that kind of behaviour. He created an atmosphere in which we, his subordinates, were ourselves prepared to take responsibility, without necessarily referring back to him every few minutes, but we knew that his advice, encouragement and, if necessary, ordinance would be available to us if and when we needed them. H's colleagues and subordinates respected him utterly, and they all felt he would stand up for the interests of the division and its people – this was the key, surely. As his followers, we *trusted* him, had *confidence* in him, and that was why we were prepared to *follow* him. Any of us would have gone to the ends of the earth for him if he had asked us to. That, quite simply, was true leadership.

By contrast, consider the case of B. whom I also encountered at a different stage of my career. This was an entirely different sort of chief executive, an individual who regarded 'leadership' as residing in taking decisions, before and aside from any consultation, and being unwilling to change any of those decisions even in the face of clear evidence that they were to say the least sub-optimal. This particular person tried to make a virtue out of inflexibility, and was even known to fly into rages if there was any dissent from decisions that had in effect been handed down. This was not leadership – it was little more than the actions of a control freak, and it was of course recognized as such by those whom the individual regarded as followers. Unlike the previous example, there was no trust, no confidence, certainly no respect and nobody would have gone anywhere near the ends of the earth for this person. Perhaps not altogether surprisingly, the ineffectiveness of this 'leader' was in fact reflected in the performance of the organization – not only was it not especially good, but many of its inadequacies were in fact subject to a significant degree of cover-up.

So it may be said that trust, confidence, and willing followership are essential to effective leadership, even though paradoxically they may manifest themselves in an apparent absence of overt leadership. Now this is extremely relevant to the non-exec's situation, because as a non-exec you are not required always to take an overt lead. There will probably be a chief executive of some sort, and he may well be sensitive to any suggestion that someone else is compromising his authority – this sort of sensitivity is especially frequently met in the smaller business. But you will tend to find that even the most apparently self-assured and self-sufficient SME chief executive looks to his non-executive colleague(s) for encouragement quite a lot, for advice surprisingly often, and even occasionally for ordinance if he finds the heat getting too much for him and wants to share, or even at times to shrug aside, some of the responsibility he bears. We will consider this phenomenon in more detail later, when looking at the roles of the non-exec as confidant and mentor, but it does seem clear that it also impinges upon the role as leader, as demonstrated above. What the non-exec really requires above all is 'charisma' in the sense recognised by Weber,[26] moral authority, the acceptance by others in the situation of his *right* to give a lead and set the agenda – the right doesn't necessarily need to be exercised to any great extent, but it does need to be there, and it does need to be acknowledged.

However, there are times when the right does in fact need to be exercised, and these are in times of crisis. Given that many SME managers and, more especially, directors, are relatively inexperienced in their very senior roles, they can sometimes appear frozen in a crisis, like a rabbit in a car's headlights. They may, quite simply, not know what on earth to do. This is when an effective non-exec will step into the breach in a major way, guiding the company perhaps through a period of technical insolvency, when nobody else is in a position to recognize what needs to be done, what can be done in practical terms, and just where and in what way the company's progress is impinged upon by matters of law, banking practice, and creditor leniency. At such times, labels like 'non-executive' don't matter – what matters is what you can do. The only caveat, perhaps, is that it would be very easy in such a situation to get 'sucked in' to the extent that the executives in effect abdicated their own responsibilities, which would not be helpful for the future of the enterprise (always supposing that you managed to secure that future). The way the effective non-exec will seek to avoid this is to take his colleagues with him, and ensure as far as possible that the journey forms part of their own development as a learning experience, so that they can themselves take control once again when the crisis is passed.

In practical terms, very often a leader's own development proceeds along with that of the organization he is leading. The effective leader will recognize that this is happening, and that it is not only desirable but in fact necessary; he will take pains to ensure that his and the organization's developments keep pace one with the other. Thus, as the kind of input required of a leader changes over time, he will be able to respond to the changes in requirements and remain as relevant and vital to the organization as he originally was. This kind of 'transformational leadership' is most definitely *not* to be mistaken for a desire to be all things to all men, rather, it is a recognition on the part of certain outstanding leaders that to remain effective and relevant they cannot risk any element of their input atrophying. It seems to match well with the 'flexibility' competency discussed in the previous chapter.

3i's definition of the non-exec role as set out in Chapter 1 included a reference to 'securing the best use of Boardroom time'. This may readily be seen as being enormously important in a small company where the directors have day-to-day hands-on management roles as well as being directors. Usually, these people are not very good at distinguishing between the two roles when it comes to agendas and discussions, so ages may be spent at board meetings discussing items of detailed operational significance which have got little to do with the overall direction of the company and to which the non-exec can in all probability make little if any contribution. So it is a good idea for a non-exec to take a lead in establishing what should and should not be included in board meeting agendas – there is nothing wrong, once you have got a good and workable format, with keeping to the same basic agenda at each meeting. It is also a good idea, however, to establish a pattern or timetable for bringing up items which don't necessarily need attention each time the board meets, such as company cars (if appropriate), pensions, dividends, salaries and perhaps capital expenditure. These can be put on a timetabled basis so that they appear automatically on the agenda at fixed intervals – quarterly, annually, or whatever – but any of them can of course be raised in between times on an ad hoc basis if there is some special requirement.

As a general rule, in a small company it is valuable to have the non-exec in the chairman's position. Not only does this offer you, the non-exec, a relatively high-profile position which carries an implied aspect of leadership, but it also offers you the chance of both influencing the agenda for board meetings – and, of course, controlling the discussion and therefore the allocation of time to items. If you are not chairman, you should make it your business to have a one-to-one session with the chairman prior to each board meeting, not to pre-empt what happens at the meeting but rather to establish what and how the best input from yourself will be. You should also ensure that, if there are any sub-committees of the board such as a remuneration committee, you are a member. (Post-Cadbury, this should be automatic, but in practice isn't always.) It is unlikely that in a small business there will be enough non-execs in place for Higgs' idea of a 'senior non-executive director' to be a realistic option, but if there are two or more then one of them should most certainly be chairman and recognized as holding a senior position.

The mentor

Mentoring is a fairly modern practice in management, though of course it has a long and worthwhile (though variable) history. It derives its name and definition from classical Greek legend – Mentor was an individual at Odysseus' court at Ithaca, tutor to his infant son Telemachus. When Odysseus went off to join the expedition to Troy, he left Mentor to be teacher, protector, counsel and friend to Telemachus. The relationship between Mentor and Telemachus was later to prove crucial when, many years after the fall of Troy, Odysseus returned from his wanderings, was at first unrecognized, and was eventually reconciled with his family.

You might at first be sceptical as to whether many managers' or directors' working environments could be compared to the Trojan War (though it must sometimes feel to them as if there are some similarities) but if you consider the lack of training or preparation many SME directors get (particularly perhaps owner–directors), and the lack in many (perhaps even 'most') SMEs of any peer group or individual peer, it is not difficult to appreciate how valuable a mentoring relationship can be. Sometimes such a thing may be obtainable from outside, and independently of, the organization: highly successful 'boardroom mentor' programmes have been run in various parts of the country, using established non-executive directors as mentors for inexperienced or would-be board members. But given the sheer numbers of SMEs, formalized programmes can only scratch the surface in terms of potential demand.

A mentor will observe what is going on; he will relate what he sees to his own experience; he will advise; he will listen to problems, to cries for help, to someone 'getting things off his chest'; he will develop a one-to-one relationship built on a unique type and style of support, being constructive rather than judgmental; and he will essentially be an *enabler*, a *facilitator*, rather than actually a *doer*. For this to work, the relationship must be a close one, and one which is sensitive to situations in a similar way to the description, in an earlier paragraph, of 'situational leadership'.

The original Mentor would not have been given his role by Odysseus had he not had credibility and trust, and in the same way you cannot expect to be effective as a boardroom mentor unless your colleagues believe in you. In part, this is a matter of empathy, as was discussed towards the end of Chapter 2, but it is also a matter of the actual relationship you manage to develop with the others on the board – this means hard work, not only in the early stages of the relationship, but also ongoing, so that your guidance is more or less automatically sought.

The 3i reference to 'giving practical and creative guidance to the directors and management of companies' is highly relevant to the role of a mentor. It may in practice mean anything from responding when asked about a particular problem or issue to actually getting your sleeves rolled up and *demonstrating* how to do something, bearing in mind that an SME may well not have a fully comprehensive skill base among its management. It is not uncommon to come up against something which is new to the company but in which it just so happens that you have some particular experience or expertise, and it may be that the best way to kick off this new thing is for you to apply your expertise in a practical sense. But it also means, in real life, that you may well have to *teach your colleagues how to be directors*. The best managers in the world won't necessarily make good directors, and indeed many of those who start up small companies haven't a clue about directorships, especially those who start up as entrepreneurs. In fact, it is by no means uncommon to find that, even where some members of a board have previously been directors – for example, when some directors of a company have staged a management buy-out from that company and have subsequently become directors of the newly bought-out company – there is still a need to ensure that ground rules are laid down for distinguishing between someone's role as a manager and their role as a director, a distinction which many new directors find very difficult to get their minds round.

So there's an element of setting and maintaining standards of conduct and performance, too. This is where you need to exercise tremendous judgement and mental subtlety. For it would be only too easy, as a mentor, to become – or be seen to become – closely involved with the board or perhaps with one or two specific members of it, and to find your objectivity compromised or suspected. This is the phenomenon of 'going native,' to which reference will be made again later. Yet at the same time, if you are to have the kind of strong and workable relationship described above, then your confidentiality and incorruptibility should never be in doubt and you should be capable of being looked on as an adviser or sounding-board for most if not all of your colleagues.

That is all very fine, but what if there is some kind of schism within the board of directors? Normally, perhaps, you should be prepared to side (if that is the appropriate word) with the person at the top, unless (as does happen from time to time) you think that he is in the wrong. For example, where a company is in severe difficulties, this may in fact be due to some measure of incompetence at the top, and the non-exec should not be afraid to blow the whistle on this if to do so would be in the best interests of the company and its stakeholders. On occasions when the other directors feel there is no alternative but to move against an MD the rest of the board will tend to look to the non-exec to give a lead in doing so, irrespective of the depth of his relationship with the individual. Indeed, there can be times when although being a mentor to the MD is a fairly significant part of a non-exec's role, the demands of situational leadership come into play and the interests of the organization take precedence over the mentorship. Life can become very lonely at such times. Clearly this isn't the sort of thing you do lightly or wantonly, but it is important to remember that even if you are acting as a mentor you are not there to be anybody's poodle, and you should be prepared to act in accordance with what you believe to be right and proper.

There is always a danger, in an SME, that a non-exec will become so closely identified with the policies and actions of the board that he will be seen as having 'gone native'. It is the author's opinion that this can be over-stated – after all, as a member of a board you must show some solidarity, otherwise you won't be at all effective. All too often, one suspects, the concept of 'going native' is applied by one shareholder (for example, an institution) whose nominee is showing unhealthily strong signs of having an independent mind. Institutions will protest that they are essentially hands-off investors, and so indeed they are . . . for most of the time, until the investee company wants to do something which isn't on the institution's wish list! Then all the fine words about hands-off and the independence of the nominee director suddenly shift in meaning and there can be some major disagreements both between the institution and the company and between the institution and the director it has nominated – in such situations there are rarely any real winners. Fortunately it doesn't seem to happen all that frequently, but there is no doubt that you have to tread a very fine line between lack of commitment and over-commitment. If in doubt, then the best advice is that you apply the test of asking the question 'is this in the interests of the shareholders as a whole or just one of them?' bearing in mind that any director's responsibility must always be to that 'whole' as far as possible.

The role of mentor is most probably of particular significance in two special types of enterprise: the new start, and the family company. In the former, as has already been suggested, you may be dealing with an individual, or for that matter with a group of people, with no previous experience of actually being where the buck stops. However confident they may be when presenting the business plan, or at the formal signing of the agreement or the investment document, they may suddenly feel awfully exposed and unsure of themselves on Day 1 of the real world, when they have to start making it all happen. If so, they are likely to need their teacher, counsel, protector and friend as never before, and your ability to relate to what they are doing, and to provide really practical guidance, could be crucial to the enterprise's success in its early days. Even if the executive/s of the new business did previously gain experience of running a company, that probably doesn't make it any less nerve-racking this time round, especially considering that this time personal financial risk is most probably involved.

In a family company, the relevance of the mentor is enhanced by the outside experience he brings to what is often (even in some quite large family businesses) an inward-looking organization. During the 1990s, I was involved with two family businesses: one run by three brothers, the other by a husband and wife. In both cases it was genuinely surprising to observe the lack of knowledge and appreciation of what went on in the world beyond the outside door; one might have thought that for the two companies to have made it as far as they had, there would have been a fairly significant element of worldliness on the part of the executives, but it didn't seem so. Much of my early input as the non-exec was therefore around the business of explaining how things actually worked in terms of supplies, payments, relations with customers, bankers and so on. I was also, at another time, a non-exec in a company where the MD's son worked in the business – he didn't have a major position in the company, but he had an opinion of himself some way ahead of his actual ability, and really if anyone needed a mentor it was he, not his father the MD.

The role of mentor does bring into sharp relief the issue of the extent to which a non-exec can, or should, place a distance or a degree of 'separateness' in the relationship between himself and the company. But it also raises an issue of just whom that relationship is with. Obviously, as a member of a board of directors you are a part of a team and you have a type of relationship with the rest of that team; but there is also, as 3i clearly recognize in their definition of the role, a special function of a non-exec to be a close and confidential adviser to the chairman and/or chief executive. This will almost inevitably place you slightly apart from the other board members, and it is right and proper both to acknowledge this and indeed to underline it from time to time. You have a special position, even although in the normal course of things you shouldn't need all that often to play the 'special' card, so there is little point in being coy and pretending otherwise. One would not expect to see a non-exec acting as mentor to any director other than the chairman or chief executive, unless it had been specifically agreed as part of his remit that he should take some responsibility for training or developing a nominated individual, and it is likely that such a remit would be extremely infrequently set. I personally have once, and once only, been asked to do this for an 'ordinary' director (that is, not the chairman or chief executive), and it did in fact prove to be an exceptionally difficult relationship to manage. More or less everywhere else it has been accepted that my relationship with the person at the top has been different from that with the rest of the board members.

The confidant

Earlier on in this work there was a reference to the issue of loneliness, when we were considering the 'psychology of the small business'. It was suggested then that the head of a small business can experience significant loneliness, and that you, the non-exec, may at times be seen by him as the only friend he has. It's perhaps surprising quite how human – and indeed how vulnerable – some MDs can be in their hopes, fears and emotions; indeed, there is an instructive quote from such an MD in an article in *The Director* magazine,[27] saying 'I didn't start out intending to bring in a non-Executive Director. I just wanted someone to talk to.' It can be a surprisingly desolate life being in charge of a smaller business, perhaps without peer colleagues, and one should never underestimate the sheer value of the opportunity for a chat – not necessarily anything as formal as a meeting or even a discussion (which tends to have some element of structure) but simply a clean-slate, blue-sky chat much of which may actually have little or nothing to do with the business or its situation but which may have an incredibly cathartic effect. It means, of course, if you're going to allow yourself to get involved, that you have to be prepared to put in the time – which very often means out-of-hours time, since that's the only way many small business managers can spare their own time. A good non-exec will, in the course of his appointments, burn enough midnight oil to fire up a small power station, just helping to preserve various MDs' sanity!

But it isn't only a case of offering a sounding-board, a shoulder to cry on, or a one-person counselling service. Quite often, an executive may be a little unsure whether a particular course of action is likely to work, even perhaps whether it's legal. To discuss it with any of his usual interlocutors, such as his colleagues, his family, or his bank manager, may at the time simply not be practical – it may set up unnecessary scares, it may be impossible to get objective opinions that way, or whatever. So the non-exec may be the one he turns to and confides in, and it is difficult to see anything wrong with that in itself.

Where it gets difficult, of course, is if there is some kind of discord within the organization and several different and possibly opposing factions seek to use you as confidant at the same time: it may be possible to use the diverse insights you get as a basis for constructing a settlement of the problem, but that is by no means certain, and if you can't construct a settlement the probability is that sooner rather than later you will find yourself somehow compromised by the sheer divergence of stances you may be being asked to support. In those circumstances, the best advice is to call a halt to the whole thing – make it clear to all concerned that it isn't constructive to go on in that way, that it isn't a worthwhile use of your time and expertise, and that ultimately it isn't doing the organization any favours. If possible, this should be done openly, in front of all the parties, in effect challenging them to behave like grown-ups! There was an occasion when I lost my cool at a board meeting of a company which had allowed its processes to get bogged down in a mire of inadequate communication; after my (rather unexpected) diatribe, nobody spoke to me for about a week, then one by one the executives came and told me how silly they reckoned they had been, how I was right in what I had said, and how they would no longer abuse my role as confidant. By and large, they kept to that resolution.

There is also an issue in this context, however, around the isolation of a non-exec. It isn't only the person in charge of a business who can find life lonely – a non-exec can also feel tremendous pressure, especially if he is (as will often be the case in a small business) the only non-executive member of the board. It could perhaps be argued that a non-exec's first appointment should as a matter of course, if possible, be to a board where there is already a non-executive chairman, so that the new non-exec also has a confidant.

The thinker

Let us be completely honest and say straight away that unless you can demonstrate a high level of intellectual capability you shouldn't even begin to contemplate becoming a non-executive director.

To say that does not, of course, mean that all non-execs must have first class honours degrees or anything like that. However, it is fairly clear that there is an element of exposing yourself in the situation, which makes it important that not only do you know what you are doing but that you also have the ability to think coherently and to relate those thoughts to what is going on around you. It is also important that you have the wit to realize both when there is congruence and when there is incongruence between thought and objective reality. In addition, you should possess a facility of expression that amply demonstrates your ability to others and enables them to share in at least some of your thoughts. Maybe that sounds like a recipe for being arrogant, but there is no need to apologize for that – all too often, there may be a knowledge gap in a small company and you may be suddenly called upon to fill it and to share the fruits of filling it.

An obvious example is in the area of strategy: business schools and gurus tell everyone how important it is, venture capital investors constantly refer to it and stress its centrality to the realization of their aims (3i recognize the role of a non-exec in helping to 'create a robust policy and strategy'), and bank managers also want to see it to underpin confidence in the managers' ability to safeguard their security. But having a strategy is something that small companies don't always do, either because they are too busy or because their directors aren't capable of thinking strategically, and in any case, for many SMEs, strategy may be summed up in a single word – survival. You may consider that perhaps a bit extreme, but the cliché about getting today right otherwise there won't be a tomorrow does hold true to a significant extent.

Having said that, however, if a company is to grow into anything more than a minnow, then it must avoid the trap of only thinking like a small company, and that means there must be a strategic focus to its plans, linked to or at least compatible with the organization's corporate values. If its executive directors are for whatever reason unable to lead on this, you the non-exec must. There will probably be many occasions when you have to challenge your colleagues on a board along the lines of 'what you're suggesting flies in the face of the philosophy/priorities/ long-term aims we identified and agreed' or 'if you carry on with such-and-such a policy we'll be in exactly the same, or worse, situation in eighteen months' time as we are now' and then explain patiently to them the incongruence between what they want and what they are heading towards getting! And you will find that in a majority of cases they will listen to you, for they will have perceived that this is in fact at least partly what you are there to do. In, probably, a majority of my own non-executive appointments I have been seen as the custodian of the organization's strategy – even if that's not how my executive colleagues might actually have expressed it.

But in a more general sense, too, intellectual skills are necessary for an SME non-exec. You may easily find yourself in a company of a type or in a sector about which you know very little. Notwithstanding what was said earlier about the benefits of matching horses and courses, there is no way anyone could absolutely guarantee that every newly-appointed non-exec was going to hit the ground running, and if you are going to make any worthwhile contribution you have to learn fast. The smaller the organization, the less likely you are to land among a large group of colleagues, and the more likely you are to have to survive on your own wits. A new non-exec in an SME will almost certainly be the sole non-exec, may well in fact constitute 50 per cent of the entire board, and is likely to find senior management thin on the ground too. He may be lucky to get any kind of induction at all, from anyone, other perhaps than a walk round being introduced to people – and there will probably be many situations where he doesn't even get that. When I became chairman of an NHS hospital trust, there were five other non-execs there whom I met for briefing sessions long before I had to attend my first board meeting: by contrast, when I became chairman of a small family-owned business the first thing I had to do was call an unprecedented board meeting and run it from scratch. There have been several references in this work to 'learning on the job', and that is often what you have to do – and in doing so, you have to be self-taught.

To be fair you should also bear in mind that SME executives may get very little 'quality time' which they can devote to thinking about things, as they may be filling several different roles at once and find a shortage of minutes in the day. It's not just strategy that doesn't get a look in: day-to-day problems tend also to get tackled 'on the hoof' without much in-depth consideration. This is a gap *you* could reason-ably be expected to fill, for you (rightly or wrongly) will be perceived as having the luxury of time! No matter that you may have a day-job, as well as your non-executive appointment, or that you may have several other non-executive appointments which also demand time and attention – to your colleagues in the company paying your fee, you are a resource to be exploited, and your powers of thought should be part of the value you add.

The doer

However, if all you do is think, it is difficult to see how you will be a great deal of use in an SME. The largest cluster in the competency study was the 'getting results' cluster, which is not in the least surprising.

As has been repeatedly stressed, you must add value, and although you may well be worth your weight in gold as a problem-solver there will almost inevitably be occasions when they need someone to *do* something – it may be to make a speech, it may be to design a procedure, it may be to get involved in a negotiation, or whatever. The really important thing is that there needs to be a recognizable *outcome* which should preferably be measurable in some way, otherwise you won't be seen or appreciated as a doer.

Now, clearly, if you can bring previous experience to bear, so much the better. For this reason, it is a good idea (i) to be quite open at the very start of your relationship with a company, and indeed from time to time thereafter, about what qualities and experience you are offering, and (ii) to keep your eyes and ears open as to what's going on, so that you can spot a breach into which you might usefully step. I have usually stressed, to prospective and new colleagues in organizations I have joined, some elements of my management consultancy background, and I have frequently been asked to get involved in issues relating to that. In one company, they knew that I had been long ago in work study, and I found myself checking a whole lot of manufacturing times for them, using a stop-watch for the first time in almost twenty years! The way they saw it, it was a great deal cheaper than engaging someone external on contract.

Where do you draw the line, though – for surely you shouldn't spend your time as a non-exec actually being part of the day-to-day operation of the company? No, obviously you shouldn't, because if you get too closely involved, you lose whatever aura you might have, and you become regarded as simply part of the organization, not anything special. So in practical terms you have to do two things. First, you have to be quite strict in terms of rationing your input. Your initial agreement with the company should have set out some parameters in terms of the amount of time you are expected to devote, and if this is in danger of being breached, you should alert your colleagues, and point out the financial implications of their having more of you. The second thing you have to do is to refer – and relate – to any agreement covering the range and scope of your proposed input: it may perhaps be necessary to discuss and agree the terms of a *project* of some kind to cover additional input.

The beauty of a *project* is that by its very nature it is finite and is pre-defined in its terms of reference and its expected deliverables. By approaching things in this way, you make it clear that although you are happy to identify closely with your executive colleagues and with the company, you are nevertheless at a slight remove and are essentially a free agent. This of course can become extremely relevant and valuable if what you have to say or do is not what people want to hear – as does indeed happen from time to time.

This is obviously an extremely difficult line to tread. The transition from thinker to doer is one you won't *necessarily* find yourself having to make, but if it is thrust upon you then you cannot simply refuse. On two occasions I found myself somewhat unexpectedly faced with the prospect of immediately taking control of a company. ('Unexpectedly' because this was not the actual role for which I had been asked to become a director in the first place, as distinct from certain other occasions when I was specifically put in as a 'company doctor'.) On each occasion I *could* have refused, but didn't. This may have been partly because problem situations were what I particularly enjoyed and was accustomed to, but it was partly also the result of a belief that if an individual is in a position to contribute, thanks to his own particular talents and people's expectations of what he might achieve on their behalf, then he has something of an obligation to apply those talents and try to achieve something worthwhile. In one of the cases just mentioned, I was able to guide the company through a period when it was technically insolvent to a satisfactory recovery, and that would not have happened, and the company would not have survived, had I not accepted the challenge. So it is argued that it is only realistic to accept that there is a subtlety and a flexibility about the non-exec role in an SME as far as the actual degree of engagement is concerned: your hands when dirty are a *special* pair of hands, not just *another* pair of hands.

The evaluator

An interesting concept to which 3i refer is what they term 'real world calibration' – by this they mean a kind of benchmarking process the non-exec is uniquely positioned to carry out, and which they describe as offering an antidote to 'dangerous feelings of invincibility and occasional delusions of competence' on the part of an organization's executives! There can sometimes be a tendency, especially perhaps if in the early days of a company's life a major success has been achieved, for the executives to be walking on air and to mistake the sensation for that of walking on water. Someone has to explain the facts of life to them, and to put things into context. Today's triumph is unlikely to be more than a single step along the way to survival for a new start, and although of course as a non-exec you mustn't dishearten your colleagues by talking down a success, you must equally ensure that they don't allow it to reduce the degree of effort they put in to meeting the next challenge along the way. So your sense of proportion is extremely important, and the extent to which you can – and can be seen to – measure and evaluate what you and others do.

Another of the qualities usually associated with, and demanded of, a non-executive director is independent judgement. You are likely to be surrounded by a lot of information (albeit of variable and perhaps unpredictable quality and accessibility . . .) and will frequently find that you have limited time and limited additional material available for decision-taking. You *may* be faced, either predictably or unpredictably, with a crisis of some sort, in which your decision or recommendation is going to be critically important. And it is entirely possible that all this may happen at a very early stage in your relationship with the particular organization.

So you need to be able to make up your mind, pretty quickly as a rule (even more so if there is a crisis or a situation of some pressure), as to where the strengths and the weaknesses are in the organization, who can be relied on and who can't, who can be developed and who can't. In an SME, these judgements are vitally important, given the likely overall shortage of people. At the same time, you may also be in a position where you have to take a view about the organization's viability as a whole. (In an ideal world, you should do this prior to accepting an appointment with the company; in the real world of the SME, this may be a counsel of perfection in that the information you need on which to base your view may simply not be immediately available and you may have to go on a 'hunch' as far as your initial liaison with the company is concerned.) If you go into a situation where there has been conflict, or other kinds of pressure, especially if your role is seen as in some way repairing things afterwards, you need to be able to take careful stock of what may perhaps be termed your 'inheritance' – various people will almost certainly bring you their own particular versions of what has happened, who are the goodies and who the baddies, and so on, and of course you will have to make up your own mind. It may have actually gone so far as to be a divided board of directors by the time you arrive, in which case it is urgent that you work out where you are going to stand. You may perhaps get some 'steer' here from the institutional shareholder, if there is one, but experience suggests that you cannot bank on getting that.

Even if the situation you go into is calm and 'normal' (whatever that is...) you still need to set out your stall regarding your views and your standards, and the standards you expect of others – especially your fellow-directors, any other key senior figures in the organization, and perhaps of relevant key external players such as the bank and any institutional shareholders. But you must also be able to recognize the main elements of the organization's culture and values (because those are also part of your 'inheritance') and to evaluate whether, or to what extent, you buy into these or need to change them. So there is really no point in being deep and unfathomable, nor is there any point in trying to be all things to all men. Your colleagues surely need to know – indeed, have a right to know – where you stand from pretty early on in the relationship, so it follows that you have to become clear in your own mind where that is. This doesn't mean being inflexible; indeed, it can be the reverse, in that what you establish is a set of basic principles or ground rules which you then use to evaluate different issues by which you are confronted, each issue being considered individually on its own merits. What it undoubtedly does mean, however, is that you need well-developed skills of judgement and must be prepared to use them.

The networker

The 3i definition of the role of the non-executive director, set out in Chapter 1, made mention of developing and using 'contacts with third parties such as financial sources, customers, suppliers, and Local and Central Government Authorities'. This is frequently cited as one of *the* most important contributions a non-exec can make to a company. It is certainly important, although one may perhaps be excused just a little cynicism about the background and motives of those who regard it as paramount. One does from time to time meet those to whom networking is so much a way of life that they do little else, and see it as an end in itself! Such persons are actually of little use to an SME, where the prime need is for practical action and added value, and where networking itself must be evaluated against criteria of practicality and added value.

There are probably two aspects to the potential value of the networker. First, you can use contacts to gain some kind of advantage for the company. This could be in terms, say, of opening a door to a potential customer or supplier whom you happen to know (but beware of the double edge this sword can have – if by some mischance one of your contacts messes things up for the other in terms of poor quality or service, you may lose two friends, not just one) or to a contact of some other kind who is able to provide an input of some sort. It could be in terms of finding sources of financial assistance; the author has, for example, been able to initiate new banking relationships, to set up some investment opportunities, and to obtain advice regarding various aspects of financial policy for companies of which he was a non-exec, thanks to the range of contacts he was able to tap into. He was also once able to set up a re-banking opportunity for a company that had fallen foul of its bank's cavalier and ignorant attitude towards small business. New starts in particular often neglect the importance of relationship-building, with the excitement of the start-up, and you can often not only do some of this, but also demonstrate its real value, quite early in your period of office.

The second aspect is less easy to define precisely or to quantify, but nevertheless it is just as real. It has to do with a company's profile and therefore what others think of it, and so it is arguably almost into the 'PR' area. An example of what is meant here is using contacts to set up new relationships which have in themselves boosted a company's credibility – for instance, moving a company's bank account from a backwater rural branch to a big city centre branch, or changing a company's auditors from an unknown local firm to a more established and well-known firm (not, it should be pointed out, one of the big and very expensive firms, for there is plenty of scope without going to that extreme), or getting a company's executives to join worthwhile networks themselves. Particularly for a company that is looking to grow, such aids to credibility can be enormously valuable, and many such companies punch above their weight partly because they are *perceived* as being in a higher weight class than they in fact are. And it is perhaps not too immodest to suggest that if you yourself have a favourable reputation in a sector or in a locality, a company might gain credibility from other people knowing that it has you as a non-executive director.

Networks exist at all levels and in relation to all manner and sizes of organization. Every locality probably has its 'mafia', which may be based round a sector (lawyers and financiers, for example, tend to be clubbable and to gravitate very much towards their own kind), or round former pupils of a particular educational establishment in the area, or round a sport organization of some kind (in many places in England there are business groups associated with the local football club, and in many Scottish towns and cities a similar phenomenon is found with rugby clubs). Of course, any such relationship must be based on, and used with, absolute probity – it's not difficult to find unfavourable stories about sport club 'mafias' and their doings, hyped by the media in much the same way as supposed 'fat cats'! But even allowing for this, it is surely perfectly legitimate in principle for a non-exec to exploit connections he has for the benefit of a company.

Probably the most important thing about networking, however, is the need to be pro-active. It is scarcely of much use to a company if your contacts have to be extracted from you like teeth. There was once a non-exec in a company which was in trouble, and he was not doing a lot apart from wringing his hands; it turned out, however, that he was well-connected locally and could in fact have provided access to some much-needed help in a particular field (in this case, property) in which the company was having problems. He said afterwards that he 'hadn't really thought it was part of his function . . . '. Another non-exec of the author's acquaintance actually tended to go to the opposite extreme – he was forever saying 'do you know so-and-so?' and trying to set up introductions. It even became a bit tiresome, in fact, but it has to be admitted that he was a much more valuable non-exec than the hand-wringer.

The terminator

In the aftermath of Cadbury, it was widely recognized that non-execs as a breed had a major role to play in upholding the principles of good corporate governance. The boundary between principles and practice, inevitably, became blurred, especially when special board sub-committees, comprising mainly or entirely non-execs, began to proliferate. A remuneration committee was seen as a potential bulwark against excessive executive plundering of a company, and a performance review committee was seen as fulfilling a similar role with regard to the abuse of managerial power. When a situation was perceived as being so dire that heads needed to roll, it became increasingly expected that the non-executive members of a board would pronounce the sentence or, at least, apply pressure for the sentence to be pronounced.

There is no reason why the same logic and expectations cannot apply to a small company as to a PLC in this area. The duty of care upon a director has been discussed in an earlier chapter, and it was pointed out that it is a universal duty which takes no account of the size or status of the organization. It has also been shown that the non-executive director is in a special position when it comes to exercising that duty of care because of the broad view he gains by virtue of being at one remove from day-to-day management issues. When it comes to matters of performance review and of heads possibly rolling, that duty stands in starker relief for being exercisable by one individual rather than by a group! But there is a strong argument which says that you should be prepared to stand up and be counted, and make quite clear your view if for example there is an issue regarding the future of another member of the board, even if that member is in fact the chief executive.

However, it is not so easy or so straightforward in a small company. For one thing, the chief executive probably has a substantial shareholding, quite possibly a majority. He may be part of a family of owners, and families do tend to close ranks around one of their members under threat. If there is an institutional shareholder, the chief executive is almost certainly someone whom the institution have consciously backed with their money, whether as a buyer-in, part of a buy-out team, a company doctor, or whatever. Now, the mere fact of being backed by institutions doesn't necessarily mean in itself that someone is any good, but doing something about the situation is not particularly easy and will require the acquiescence of the relevant institution/s – and institutions don't much enjoy admitting they are wrong. If you get rid of the chief executive, who will take his place? There may be no obvious successor within the organization, and it's not easy to recruit chief executives for SMEs.

Even allowing for all that, however, it is sometimes necessary to invoke the doctrine of 'the greater good'. It happened to the author with three chief executives in ten years; it was not particularly enjoyable, and not something any normal human being could ever get used to or acquire a taste for, but when it came to the crunch there was no realistic alternative.

The curious thing is that, in two of the three cases, it was not a surprise to the chief executive. Both these two went relatively quietly – in fact, one of them actually said he reckoned his number was up almost before the non-exec had opened his mouth. Because getting rid of a director is such an extreme measure (still more so a chief executive), things have to be pretty bad for it to be necessary, and it would be an extraordinarily blind director (and an even more blind chief executive) who didn't see how bad things were. In the two instances mentioned above, everyone was aware that the company was in serious trouble and it had become apparent that the departure of the man at the top was a 'when' issue, not an 'if' issue.

The third case, however, was not linked with poor company perform-ance – or at least, not in an immediate sense. The problem was one of conflict in the boardroom, and the roots of the conflict lay in the personality and behaviour of the chief executive. There had been previous conflict before the author had been a member of that board, and the company had lost a great deal of money in a year during which most of the other directors had resigned because they just couldn't work any longer with the chief executive. With the new non-exec's help and guidance, some stability was restored and profits had returned, but fresh appointees to the board had in due course fallen out with the chief executive just as their forebears had done – but unlike their forebears they had expressed a determination not to resign but to stand and fight from within for what they saw as the future of the company. It developed into an irreconcilable situation, from which the only rational way out seemed to the non-exec to be the departure of the chief executive, for it really did appear that there was an element of inevitability that he would fall out with whoever were his executive colleagues, and such repeated breakdowns were clearly damaging to the company and its stakeholders.

The chief executive himself, of course, didn't see it like that, so there was no way he was going to go quietly. This of course necessitated a great deal more work than the other two departures mentioned above, because all the legal implications had to be followed through, together with infinitesimal analysis of the company's articles of association, so that the action taken against him could be watertight. In the end, as it happened, it wasn't watertight, but its 'leak' occurred in a totally unexpected place which was not in fact part of the boardroom conflict as such – a minor shareholder among the company's management, who was not a member of the board but was perceived with good reason as being no admirer of the chief executive, totally against the run of play sided with him and in so doing guaranteed him a majority of voting shares.

Leaving aside for the moment the question of outcomes, however, what is significant about all three cases above is that in each case the non-executive director was expected to be a prime mover in the chief executive's removal. It certainly wasn't a question of unilateral action, for in each case the entire board was united in its opposition to the chief executive and in its desire to see him go, but in each case the non-exec's active agreement and participation were seen as absolutely necessary. From his own point of view, in each case what *he* saw as absolutely necessary was a board united in its support of the proposed course of action, as well as support of the institutional investors (each of the three companies had them) and an agreed programme of telling the employees and other key players (bankers, key customers, key suppliers, and so forth) as soon afterwards as practicable what had been done, why, and what was now proposed as a way forward. None of this was substantially different, other than in terms of scale, from what would be expected of non-execs in a post-Cadbury PLC.

While on the subject of terminations, one should make the point that it is important to allow an individual to leave with dignity – unless, of course, there's been some wrong-doing. In large companies, a terminated chief executive will often leave with a very full wallet, something which tends to be seen as a bit of fat-cattery. This can – and indeed has – become a major issue in times of economic slowdown when profitability and stock-market value are declining and there is an attrition among senior executives of failing companies, and it is another issue that generates far more heat than light. Suffice it to say for the present that although it can admittedly be galling to think that someone who has manifestly been unsuccessful (in some cases, almost spectacularly so...) receives what seems to be a huge pay-off, it may be that the individual is on a fixed-term contract, in which case there is most probably an entitlement to some compensation, and perhaps in reality it is to the initial terms of the contract that corporate as well as public attention ought to be paid, rather than to the terms of its ending. In an SME, however, it is most unlikely that there is scope for any kind of 'golden goodbye', and the dignity or otherwise of the parting may rest with non-monetary aspects, such as what the employees, customers, bankers, and so on are told. If there are any relatively low-cost things that can be done, such as allowing an MD to hang on to his company car for a limited period, there seems no *prima facie* reason not to do so.

Mercifully, the need to terminate doesn't occur all that often. When it does, however, notwithstanding how unpleasant the experience may be, the non-exec ought to be there, acting on behalf of the company and its stakeholders. If you can't cope with that, don't be a non-exec. Moreover, if you can't cope with it *on your own*, without close colleagues for mutual support, don't be an SME non-exec.

It's not just a question of getting rid of fellow directors, either. In a very small business, the non-exec may be asked by the executives to do all manner of dirty work for them, quite apart from any boardroom reshuffle which might be indicated. R. was once helping a new start as a non-exec, and it was agreed that they needed to recruit a salesman. During the start-up process, the executives had used the services of a firm of marketing consultants who advised on aspects of creating and promoting the brand. They had a fairly long-standing contact in the firm, and the consultants had given them a good deal in financial terms regarding the work they carried out, so they asked the firm if they could help in finding a suitable salesman – perfectly logical and sensible. However, the person who was taken on turned out, after a few weeks, to have a serious drink problem, and it transpired that the marketing consultants had in fact known this but had not told the directors about it. The two executive directors were most embarrassed: they felt – rightly – that they had been shafted, but because of the relationship with the firm and a particular individual within it they had a bit of a problem in knowing quite how to handle the situation. So they asked R. what he thought, and he said that on balance he believed the relationship had been fatally undermined and that they should sack the marketing consultancy firm as advisers. This was clearly going to be difficult for the executives to do, so R. offered to do it and they accepted his offer with relief. R. managed to effect the parting in a reasonably non-acrimonious manner, but the consultants were nevertheless left in no doubt as to how much damage the company felt had been done. A non-exec who had not been prepared to assume the role would not have been much use.

The mole

Perhaps it's unfair to describe this as a *bona fide* role of a non-exec. However, it has been highlighted because it can certainly be a perceived role, in which case arguably some hard work is required to overcome the perception. It only really comes to the fore when you are put on to the board of a subsidiary by a parent company, or when you serve as a nominee, say of an investing institution, and even then it may never actually become an issue, although it may be part of what you're there to do.

The author has served as an institutional nominee, for various different institutions, on the boards of nine investee companies, and has found it a matter of intense interest to watch and monitor the attitude of his colleagues towards the relationship between him and the institutions! To a fairly large extent, and not surprisingly, it has been dependent on the kind of relationship between the company itself (as represented by the rest of its board) and the institution; if the relationship has been strong and positive, the nominee non-exec has usually been seen as a potential asset, whereas if there has been tension or suspicion in the relationship then he has been seen as a 'plant' of some kind, a sort of fifth columnist who will report everything that is said and done straight back to his institutional masters.

So, to start with, the view that is taken of the institutionally-nominated non-exec is not necessarily a matter within his control. The point was made in an earlier chapter that the fault may just as easily lie with the company or with the institution itself in terms of one perhaps not making its agenda clear or explicit enough and the other perhaps forgetting or ignoring just why an investment has been made in the first place. An effective institutional nominee non-exec will make it his business to work to clear up misunderstandings of this sort, through the kind of regular and focused communication network that tackles such issues at as early a stage as possible, perhaps (and ideally) even before they have had the chance to become issues. He will work to ensure that he is not seen as just representing the interests of one shareholder, while at the same time recognizing, and helping his executive colleagues to recognize, that an investing institution is looking to make money – that is its business, and to pretend that it is some kind of benevolent organization, laying out cash because it enjoys it, is just plain stupid. Yet it's amazing how many directors of 'investee' companies seem to have that view. Any such tendency must be nipped in the bud.

Common sense demands that the first priority must surely be to ensure that all parties understand what the appointment is all about – why you're there, what you will be doing, to whom you will be reporting, and what you will be reporting to them. It's equally important to be up-front about this to your 'nominator' as it is to your new colleagues, and there is a strong argument for believing that both those parties have an equally reciprocal obligation to you to be up-front about what they see as the priorities, what they expect of you, and indeed how they tend to view your relationship with the other party. This kind of systematic approach to the appointment and use of non-execs is much more likely to be found in the big corporation than in the SME – but that doesn't make it right for the SME to try to do without it. As was suggested in Chapter 2, a small company that wants to grow should try to behave like a scaled-down version of a big company, and a major aspect of that has to be to systematize the way it does things. It may well be one of the major contributions you make as a non-exec if you can bring about a transformation in its approach and operating methodology.

At the same time, it is also important to remember the two-way nature of the flow of information and opinion. Investing institutions have been around for quite a long time, and like any long-established organizations can get somewhat set in their ways; it is arguable that their officers have in some instances a rather narrow background and training when it comes to the potential to understand practical management issues. An investment controller in an institution probably quite genuinely *does not know or understand* many of the issues being dealt with by an investee company's management, and that's not meant to be a criticism of individual controllers (although it is something of a criticism of institutions more generally). But there is no valid reason why a controller should not be able to regard the nominee non-exec as a two-way conduit for information about respective wishes, hopes and fears, priorities, and so on, and equally there is no valid reason why either the company or the investor should be afraid of this. Note, however, the deliberate use of the words '*should* be afraid', because it's something of a counsel of perfection which doesn't by any means always apply in practice!

But in just the same way as a good non-exec can make a difference to the way a company operates, he can also make a difference to the relationship with investors. It's partly about setting a good example in conduct and communication, and as part of that insisting that others follow the same high standards that you yourself set. Being an effective director is all about safeguarding interests, and it was made clear in Chapter 1 that there are a range of interests all of which must be looked after. If you believe that an institution is undermining an interest or set of interests and requiring you to be party to that undermining, you should raise the issue with the investment controller, and be prepared to take the matter higher if you do not think it has been dealt with satisfactorily. Now, let us not be under any illusions – this may cost you your appointment! The author knows of cases where such circumstances cost a non-exec any further appointments, but it was something that a particular individual felt very strongly about and he arguably would not have wished for further appointments under similar circumstances of what he saw as inappropriate institutional conduct. On the other side of the coin, many non-execs (including the author) have also sometimes found themselves being very critical of how a company is behaving towards its institutional investor, and have tried to use what influence they had to change this. Once again, it is ultimately a question of whether something is in the interests of the shareholders as a whole, or whether one man's benefit is another man's detriment. If it's the latter, then it really doesn't matter whose nominee you are or what the rest of the relationship is like – you are 'independent' and should act as such.

On the specific question of holding shares, it has occasionally been suggested that companies should consider paying their non-execs at least partly in shares rather than in cash. This is far from convincing as a principle, for two main reasons. First, it is something of a potential 'cop-out' – directors really should be paid for what they do and that payment should be of a defined and predictable value, not subject to the vagaries of a company's fortunes which may not be wholly related to its true performance. Second, one suspects it could to some extent compromise independence, particularly in a small company with very few shareholders to start with – the non-exec would have an axe to grind in just the same way as his executive colleagues, and might, just might, risk losing sight of the existence of stakeholders who were not also shareholders. However, for the present let it just be said that reservations about being *remunerated* in shares do not constitute an objection to the idea of a non-exec *holding* shares, and moreover 3i's use of the adjective 'independent' does not seem in any way to preclude a non-exec holding shares.

However, what it almost certainly does preclude is a non-exec being there, and acting, as a representative of a particular shareholder to the possible exclusion or detriment of other shareholders. You may think this is an obvious point, and to some extent so it is – but can a director who has been nominated, and whose appointment is enshrined as a right, by a particular shareholder ever be (or be seen as) truly independent? Indeed, the author has sat at a meeting and been told by a venture capital investment controller that he and his colleagues, as nominee directors, were on boards to safeguard the interests of that particular institutional investor. Many of those present felt distinctly uncomfortable about this, believing that it could easily lead to schism and doubt in boardrooms, to say nothing about any legal implications. The same kind of issue could in fact quite possibly arise also with 'business angels' who, with the best will in the world, must inevitably regard at least part of their function as being to maximize their return. Yes, one accepts that in doing so they are also likely to maximize the return that other shareholders get, as well, but as with almost any outside investor an 'angel' is looking for specific returns within a defined (and usually fairly limited) timescale, and that is a particular agenda which is bound to be high in his consciousness or in that of his nominee on an investee company's board.

In the real world there are times, in companies where there is a non-executive nominee of an investor, when there are in effect two board meetings: the official one, with the non-exec there, and a more shadowy one (usually a day or so beforehand) at which the other directors discuss anything they don't want him to hear, or anything where they want to present a united front at the official board meeting, so that by the time he is around there is an agreed 'party line' or, at least, no public disagreement among the executive directors. Everyone knows it goes on, and there is in reality very little the non-exec can do about it, other than to insist that everything that is crucial to the progress of the company finds its way on to the agenda of the official board meeting where it is thoroughly discussed and minuted. The reason for the apparent duplicity, in many instances, is not so much a mistrust of the non-exec himself, but rather a perception that, as the institutional nominee, he isn't an insider and isn't perhaps totally independent, and might just possibly need to work to a slightly different agenda if push came to shove.

In an owner-managed business, there is always the possibility that an institutional nominee may be seen as a 'mole' for the institution, however much that may be an unrealistic and unfair perception. In all probability, it arises in part from a basic naiveté on the part of the owner–managers who sometimes do not fully understand where the institution is coming from and what it is looking for in such matters as financial return, means and timing of exit, and so on; but it's only fair to say that in part it can be the institution's own fault for perhaps not explaining fully at the outset what its intentions and requirements are. It also has to be said that institutions or their representatives do behave badly at times, for example when a sale-based exit is being negotiated or when an investee company is in difficulties; by 'behave badly' is meant act in such a way as to seriously undermine the owner–managers' confidence in the particular institution. Indeed, occasions arise where an institution will indicate to a nominee director how he is expected to act, and will indicate displeasure if he dares to act differently – independence, then, can be a relative term.

Hands-how-far-off?

It must surely be clear by now how important it is that non-execs in SMEs are not there just to observe, monitor or comment. Adding real value in the SME context has, as has hopefully been shown, an immediacy which demands that their role is not only pro-active but also engaged. In other words, the 'nodding donkey' is not just undesirable, he is positively harmful.

But at the end of the day, it does appear that we have to try to balance two apparently irreconcilable requirements – the need to be involved, and the need to maintain an element of distance or aloofness in the relationship between the non-exec and the company. In the context of the SME, neither of these can be ditched in favour of the other, because it's only by being involved that you can achieve anything worthwhile in an SME, and it's only by being somewhat detached that you achieve and preserve authority and influence as a non-exec.

Are they truly irreconcilable? Is it not perhaps more likely that the ability to find and activate the balance between them is the true mark of the effective non-exec, and that this is the real summation of all the distinguishing competencies explored in Chapter 3 and all the roles discussed in this chapter?

Research conducted in 1993–4 by the University of Paisley and the Centre for Leadership Studies at the University of Surrey looked in some detail at the ways in which non-executive directors influenced the proceedings and decisions of companies' boards.[28] At the same time, attention was given to the issue of whether SMEs needed the sort of input non-execs could provide. Interestingly, one outcome of the research was to highlight the danger that non-execs might become too involved in their company's routine decision-making, a danger to which attention has been drawn once or twice in this book. However, the researchers did nevertheless suggest that part of a non-exec's effectiveness might lie in his ability 'to discern how far and how often to become involved in executive management'. There was in other words a realization that there can be times when it just is not enough to expect others to perform, and that it is knowing when to step into the breach that really helps to identify the exceptional performer. What is particularly interesting about this observation is that it is specifically related to SMEs; it is not just an attempt to downsize and then cut-and-paste onto SMEs something which clearly applies to large organizations. As such, it clearly has a head start in the validity stakes.

Some of the case studies selected for Part II of this book turn crucially around the degree of a non-exec's involvement in a company's executive management, and as both successful and unsuccessful examples of directorships are included it may well be possible to analyse whether in each case the non-exec got that degree of involvement right or not. Detailed analysis of the case studies will tend to lead to the conclusion that there are not really any 'absolutes' in terms of appropriate degrees of involvement. The author's own experience includes highly successful non-executive stints which could be described almost as 'classical' in that they were hands-off, strategically focused, and never anywhere near the operational end of the management spectrum, and equally successful stints which have been so hands-on that the non-exec has become more or less fused to the company. There have also been instances which have quite suddenly taken a turn from being at one extreme to being at the other, and it simply is not accurate to say that the success or otherwise has depended on the position on the spectrum – except insofar as the non-exec has proved capable of acting appropriately to the requirements placed upon him.

So, ultimately, the recommendation is for a totally flexible approach to the question of whether the hands should be 'on' or 'off', depending on the circumstances; but it is important to make the point that such a recommendation carries with it a very strong argument for the validity and legitimacy, in appropriate situations, of a hands-on non-exec role in SMEs.

Horses, courses, and universality

The thrust of this book has been as far as possible to relate the identification and discussion of roles in the above paragraphs to the practicalities of life in SMEs as experienced by real-life non-execs, and it is quite interesting to measure it against what came out of the 'competency' evaluation examined in Chapter 3. There certainly does appear to be some significant level of correlation between the roles described above and the competencies identified as 'distinguishing' – all the roles, it may be argued, are closely compatible with at least some of the competencies, while that of mentor seems to link with all five distinguishing competencies. Although models can all too readily appear somewhat facile, putting the roles and the distinguishing competencies into the matrix shown in Table 4.1 does help to demonstrate and highlight those relationships.

Table 4.1   Role/Competency Correlation

	Initiative	Strategic influencing	Self-development	Positive self-image	Flexibility
Leader	x	x		x	x
Mentor	x	x	x	x	x
Confidant		x	x		x
Thinker	x	x	x	x	
Doer	x			x	x
Evaluator		x			x
Networker	x	x	x	x	
Terminator	x			x	x
Mole	x	x		x	

The model doesn't attempt to 'rank' either the roles or the competencies in order of importance, nor does it rank in any order the particular competencies identified as relating to any specific role. No doubt such an exercise could be done, but it is hard to see how it would add an awful lot to the argument because, in all probability, all that it would tend to do would be to narrow down some of the correlations to an extent that would unnecessarily restrict the pool in which one could go fishing for non-execs.

What the model does is to illustrate that there appears on the face of it to be a good deal of correlation as far as attributes and activities are concerned – but what about sectors? So far in the book, little emphasis has been placed on sectoral issues, with more coverage given to what non-execs do rather than the sectors they do it in. How important, at the end of the day, is sector knowledge or experience?

At the last count, the author reckoned he had served as a director of more than thirty organizations. The range of sectors has been wide – six professional services companies, five companies in engineering and related fields, four in clothing, three in home improvements, three in the area of advertising and marketing, and two in food and drink, as well as one each in metal stockholding, plastic recycling, office supplies, storage, filling stations, car washes, fish farming, plus an NHS Trust and a Health Board. Adopting a different way of differentiating, you could say ten manufacturing companies, ten service companies, and something of a hotch-potch of others!

Whichever way one looks at it, it's a pretty diverse list. But the same sorts of issues, problems and opportunities have tended to crop up again and again right across all these organizations: management and organizational development, short-term financial viability and cashflow, interaction of people, striking the balance between cost and quality or level of service, and so on. And the decision-taking process, although of course reflecting the way each organization is structured, has tended to have many of the same characteristics each time, in terms for example of the relative strengths of individuals' personalities, the financial implications of the issue, the extent to which the decision-takers are practically experienced, or the extent to which they are in reality in control of their own destinies as distinct from being beholden to an outside third party.

Here we are approaching the true heart of the matter. Suppose an individual is in a position of responsibility in an organization – let's say, a manufacturer of components of some kind. If that individual's job function revolves round the actual manufacturing process, he may well become something of a genius in the context of material utilization, pressing, assembling, batch controlling, and all the other bits which go to make up the specialism in which he works. But his genius may or may not be transferable. There are many similarities between the sort of manufacturing environment just described and, for example, the manufacture of clothing, but at the operational level it would not be very usual to find a 'genius' in one becoming equally valuable in the other. On the other hand, it is less unusual to find senior managers in one type of company succeeding in another type, because what they are transferring is a less sector-specific range of skills; a similar point might in passing be made for functional specialists such as accountants and HR people. The argument is, therefore, that the transferability of skills is a vital element in the effectiveness of a non-exec, for if your skills are so specialized that they are not really transferable then you are likely always to be working at a level of detail which is appropriate only for an executive, and you are most unlikely to be capable of 'standing back' and confronting the kinds of issues, problems, and opportunities which were referred to in the previous paragraph.

Consequently, it is not very likely that you will find many manufacturing process geniuses among the ranks of non-execs – or, for that matter, many accounting geniuses or many HR geniuses. But equally, you are unlikely to find very many of those sorts among *executive* directors either, because what makes them good at what they do would not tend to make them good directors, of either type. In Chapter 1, an attempt was made to sketch out what differentiated the function of a director from that of a manager – principally, the characteristics and levels of accountability – and it is probably true to say that, on the whole, the more specialized, the more narrowly-focused, the more of an enthusiast a person is in the job he does, the less likely he is to be comfortable with the sorts of accountability a director has to take on. Indeed, one could perhaps go further, and suggest that the 'specialized', the 'narrowly-focused', and the 'enthusiast' are not in fact likely to figure at all in the matrix above. Now it is important to be clear that this is not an argument for *generalist* skills as opposed to *specialist* skills, but it most certainly is an argument – and a strong plea – for *transferable* skills.

If we accept, then, that as a rule directors need transferable skills, is it possible in this context to differentiate between executives and non-executives? Possibly only in matters of degree. In other words, someone who is an effective executive director is *more likely* (but, it must be recognized, by no means certain) to make an effective non-executive director than someone who is ineffective as an executive director – but it isn't an *absolute* standard and it certainly isn't a sufficient criterion. However, one does have the impression that there tends to be more variety, and less predictability, about what a non-exec gets involved in compared to his executive counterpart, and this heightens and increases the importance of transferability of skills and, incidentally, the need to bear this in mind in any selection process.

Finally, on the subject of transferability, we must come back to what is arguably the key feature of SMEs – their lack of a rich seam of management. Because of this lack, it surely must be accepted that a non-exec will inevitably find himself at some stage or other becoming engaged in things to a degree that simply wouldn't happen in larger organizations. Adaptability and flexibility really are crucial to being able to add value, and skill transferability surely lies at the heart of most of the roles that have been described in this chapter, as well as of most of the distinguishing competencies.

If the 'universal SME non-exec' fits our matrix, who is he? Is there in effect a cohort from among whom he should ideally be recruited?

This could be dangerous ground! One could make all sorts of enemies by, for example, ruling out of serious consideration whole swathes of people because of their age, background, experience, and so on, to say nothing of the equal danger of creating or seeming to create an unrealistically narrow 'cohort' which if adhered to by those seeking and appointing non-execs might in fact deprive businesses of the services of countless extremely valuable and possibly potentially life-saving individuals. However, it has been said, and hopefully demonstrated, that being an effective non-exec in an SME isn't easy, and if we are to accept that then it naturally follows that we must advocate at least some measure of selectivity.

Clearly, there are some selection criteria that virtually propose themselves. The need for intellectual ability has already been convincingly demonstrated. A degree of experience at senior level in an organization is also necessary, together with experience of operating as a director or, at the very least, operating closely with directors (as for example some management consultants might do). Experience in more than one organization, and more than one *type* of organization, is also arguably so valuable as to be just about essential, and added to this may be a need to have experience in more than one *sector*. Bearing in mind the various characteristics and qualities peculiar to SMEs, one might tend to see it as essential for an SME non-exec to have had at least some previous exposure to or experience in an SME, although as was hinted in an earlier chapter it is also valuable for an SME non-exec to be capable of understanding what goes on in larger organizations so that in the event that an SME wants to grow he can help it to grasp some of the key points about larger company behaviour and operation.

Usually, though not unexceptionally, generalists rather than specialists make the better non-execs, as was hinted above, and this is almost certainly more pronounced and more applicable in smaller organizations. However, a note of caution may be appropriate here. By 'generalists' are meant mainly those who are operating in a management environment where the predominant skills required are those found in general management as distinct from those associated with a functional specialism, but this doesn't preclude individuals whose initial training and experience may have been in such a functional specialism – so it's what they are *doing* and what they are *achieving* that counts, not necessarily what they were originally trained in. Having said that, however, the case has previously been made against those who are extremely specialized becoming directors, whether executive or non-executive – in other words, while you may start out in some specialism you need to move in a generalist direction if you're to acquire any potential value as a non-exec. Nevertheless, it is obvious that whatever else you may have in the way of attributes you must have a high degree of financial awareness and tremendous inter-personal skills.

There is a controversial issue of whether the use of retired individuals as non-execs is appropriate. Personally I would tend to argue against it, on the grounds of energy reserves and up-to-date thinking – like it or not, it must be accepted that most people slow up somewhat and become less imaginative thinkers when they reach retirement age. Taking a stand like this is, clearly, likely to infuriate a number of extremely energetic and sharp-witted sexagenarians, and of course there will always be exceptions. Very well, then, let there be exceptions, and let those exceptional individuals exploit their rarity, but in the end it should be recognized that they *are* exceptions. Similarly, some of those who retire early may do so because for financial reasons they no longer need to work, and care needs to be exercised with them too – in terms of the motivation that drives them (for what you most certainly don't want is a dilettante non-exec), in terms of the level of commitment to the enterprise they are prepared to demonstrate, and in terms of their own commitment to keeping abreast of management thinking, skills, and the statutory context. Moreover, someone who is no longer at the heart of business will tend to drop out of some of the key business networks, and the importance of networks has been highlighted more than once in this work.

In many respects, therefore, the 'ideal' SME non-exec is likely to be someone who is still in a job, at a senior level, who somehow or other manages to find the time to devote to assisting one or more other organizations apart from the one which actually employs him. This may be a bit like looking for hens' teeth, and pre-supposes a substantial degree of forbearance on the part of such a person's colleagues and superiors! However, there are plenty of self-employed consultants and similarly-oriented individuals who in fact have both the time and the capability to fill the role, and nowadays it is not uncommon to find such individuals grouped together in partnerships or even limited companies (the author in fact was part of such a company for a number of years in the late 1980s and early 1990s.) The principal advantage of such people is that they tend to be extremely results-driven, and because they are in their own way 'professionals' just as accountants, lawyers, and so on are, they take the trouble to establish and maintain their reputations, and are motivated at least partly by the need and desire to do so. Their self-confidence will tend to be high, and they will tend to have personal credibility – both these, certainly, are important for a successful non-exec. Their other significant advantage is likely to be their independence – because most of them will not depend totally on a particular directorship for their income, they will be more likely to meet the criteria for independence discussed in Chapter 1. The danger, if such it is, would be that those operating in a primarily consultancy-type environment might fail to recognize the difference between that and the environment of the non-exec, particularly in terms of the ongoing nature of the non-exec's role in an organization, and perhaps therefore pay less attention then they might to the building and nurturing of longer-term relationships.

In the end, however, there is almost bound to be a significant element of luck in whether or not there is a real 'fit' between an individual non-exec and a company. It's not just a matter of roles or competencies – personal chemistry is extremely important and should without doubt be accorded a great deal of weight. The author once had a consultancy colleague who used to say 'don't work with people you don't like', and he was absolutely right. Granted, it's not always possible to choose your colleagues, but (particularly if you are in a situation of some stress) if the chemistry isn't right then it's very likely that it will all end in tears. Anyone analysing his own successes and failures during his career will probably conclude that the greatest of the former have coincided with situations where the interpersonal relationships were good, and the greatest of the latter with situations where they were not so good. Perhaps this too suggests a need for more attention to be paid to the selection processes for non-execs.

We seem to live nowadays in an age of easy answers – or at least, an age which wants easy answers: sound-bytes rule OK. If you can sum up the totality of human knowledge and understanding on a particular subject in a few sentences, then good for you – you have a future as an expert. But, of course, the word 'expert' means someone who has tried his hand at something, it doesn't necessarily mean he's any good at it. The world is full of pontificators, but one of the best antidotes to this lies in the aphorism: those who can, do; those who can't, talk about it – or devise models, in an attempt to standardize or universalize something the diversity of which they are incapable of comprehending, still less of describing or explaining.

So this book does not try to lay down a comprehensive model for an SME non-exec. This is not a cop-out: in truth, there may not be such a phenomenon as a 'universal' SME non-exec. It does come down to horses for courses – but hopefully it has been demonstrated that the courses aren't totally straightforward or necessarily predictable, and that the choice of horses needs to be an informed one. One may hope, also, that the field from which such a choice is made is a little clearer, and a little more open to that process of choice, for what has been set out in this book.

Summary of key points

- High performance from a non-exec comes when four key factors overlap: knowledge, skills, experience and competencies.
- Although there is clearly a need for something more practical and pragmatic than a model, there are a number of roles which non-execs are likely to have to perform at one time or another which, together, offer a kind of structure within which individuals may be evaluated.
- The key roles are those of the leader, the mentor, the confidant, the thinker, the doer, the evaluator, the networker, the terminator and the mole.
- A substantial part of a non-exec's effectiveness may lie in the degree of pro-activeness with which he fulfils these roles, and in his ability to stand back or to get involved as appropriate.
- A significant correlation may be demonstrated between the roles identified above and the distinguishing competencies from Chapter 3. The

congruence may be more closely – and causally – related to a non-exec's effectiveness than any specific sector-based experience, for effective directors need skills which are transferable between different sectors. If anything, this transferability is even more important for non-execs than for executives.

- Although it is clearly dangerous to attempt to define too narrowly a 'cohort' from which effective SME non-execs should be recruited, some suggested benchmarks include:
  – intellectual ability
  – experience of operating as a director or at least working closely with directors
  – experience in more than one organization, more than one type of organization, and more than one sector
  – in most cases, generalist ability and experience rather than specialist
  – in most cases, being in work (and needing to work) rather than being retired.

- Quite apart from all this, however, the 'fit' in terms of personal chemistry must be right between a non-exec and his executive colleagues. (A good axiom is 'don't work with people you don't like.') Horses and courses should match: and the choice of horse needs to be an informed one which takes into account the peculiarities of the course.

PART II

Practical Applications

5
Background to Case Histories

So far in this book the tendency has been towards the theoretical, although an effort has been made wherever possible to illustrate points with practical examples. However, it is obviously one thing to appreciate what *should* be done, and quite another to *do* it. All the theory – indeed, all the knowledge and understanding – in the world will only be of use if it can be effectively applied, and simply possessing the theory, or the knowledge, or the understanding does not in any way guarantee that the possessor is capable of such application. So it is time to confront the real world of the SME boardroom – or, to be more accurate, the SME general office, since many SMEs don't have the luxury of a separate boardroom and much of what goes on does so in a relatively open forum.

My own first non-executive directorship appointment was as the nominee of an investing institution which I had been courting. The company was in fact a new start, and in all honesty it would have to be said that I was 'learning on the job' – but so were the three founder-directors of the particular company, none of whom had previously had positions at board level, so to an extent everyone was in the same situation.

The company in question was an advertising agency, which wasn't a type of business I knew much about, but in fact the essentials of new business survival turned out to be pretty universal. My main role was to provide advice and reassurance on aspects of running a business, such as monitoring profit contribution per job, judging staff requirements and performance, and trying to use my own network of contacts to open doors to potential clients. The 'strategy' (such as it was) was really little more than day-to-day survival, and one would hardly call the business, or indeed my contribution to it, especially sophisticated. The first couple of years were hair-raising at times, with the three working directors having to do more or less every job in the place – not here the luxury of delegation, at least not for some time, until the company and its organization structure grew sufficiently for that to become practicable. Fortunately, however, they had the advantage of being extremely good, especially on the creative side, and highly thought of in the advertising business, so they were able to bring in work when it really mattered. As they grew in maturity and confidence, so did their non-exec, so that by the time I came off their board, after five years, both the company and I were unrecognizable from the time of the start. With hindsight, it has to be admitted that both the institution and the company took a pretty enormous gamble with my appointment, and in a sense of course so did I; but on the other hand there has to be a starting-point somewhere, and so presumably the view was that I had a reasonable pedigree and so was unlikely, on balance, to do much harm. An approach such as that may not be 'elegant', in terms of textbook standards and models, but sometimes it is all there is, and at least if it works it can always be justified in retrospect...

Over a subsequent period of a dozen years or so, the range of my work took me into contact with companies under a wide range of circumstances including start-ups, buy-outs, rescues, structural change and sometimes last rites. I had a number of non-executive appointments myself, and was a close witness to many more while working in some other advisory capacity. Some were straightforward, some unpredictable, some frankly bizarre; none was boring. Some were successful in that the companies prospered, some were successful in that an agenda about something other than prospering was safely delivered, and some were not successful. I myself lived through two receiverships and a liquidation, and it was not a pleasant experience. Despite the positive efforts of receivers and liquidators, generally humane and conscientious people, one tends to end up feeling almost dirty, especially if 'on parade' at a creditors' meeting; if one has been working one's socks off trying to keep a business afloat it can in fact be quite galling. And, of course, there is always the possibility that the people at the DTI – who, without wishing to impugn the professionalism of civil servants, can hardly be expected to know or understand all that much about the day-to-day realities of running a business, and whose approach seems to be more that of 'ticking the boxes' than of a qualitative or even quantitative evaluation of how an ultimately unsuccessful business has been run – will set in motion their rather secretive processes through which they decide that such-and-such an individual is 'unfit' to be a director. (Unlike most of our justice system, in this context you are presumed culpable and the onus is very much on you to prove otherwise.)

It would be good to think that a non-exec – and indeed any other advisor – learns something from each experience in which he is involved. Many probably relive in their minds, countless times, particular episodes or even entire appointment spans, often wondering if things might have turned out otherwise had they acted differently; that probably applies no less to 'successful' appointments than to 'unsuccessful' ones. For it is surely important to understand that things very rarely go *all* right or *all* wrong – even in a successful situation, there will almost certainly be aspects which give cause for regret or which could in some way have been very much better, and the converse applies in unsuccessful situations.

With that in mind, eight episodes involving the activities of non-executive directors have been selected for analysis here. The principal criterion for selection has been whether or not there is a story to tell, rather than whether or not it is a success story! Four were (to varying degrees) successful in terms of company performance, four were not. Of the four which were not successful, one could perhaps be said to have shown a degree of success in terms of the non-exec being instrumental in delivering an agenda, and in all four there were partial or incidental successes along the way, things which went right and perhaps mitigated slightly what might seem like failure at the end of the day, and at least bear out some of the theories on which this book is based. The selection is perhaps somewhat skewed towards situations where the non-exec was a nominee of institutional investors, but that is in fact coincidental and it is probably realistic to claim that the eight, taken as a whole, are representative of the 'canon' of work of a great many non-executive directors.

The cases are all totally factual, and the point should be made that each is complete within itself – unlike some reference works, where case studies are in fact amalgams of several different situations put together for the sake of making or emphasizing a particular point, each case study here relates to one company or group, each covers one unbroken period of time, and each represents the experience of one individual non-executive director. They are presented in narrative form, trying to be as honest as possible about what individuals did or did not do, and should or should not have done; there is an attempt wherever relevant to relate what happened, and what the non-exec in the particular case did, to the principles and roles discussed in Part One of the book. At the end there are conclusions drawn about the practicality or otherwise of the 'universal' considerations highlighted in Chapter 4. Whether it all stacks up must, however, be for the individual reader to decide.

6

Heavy Engineering Company

This case is an excellent illustration of what a non-executive director of an SME may unwittingly be letting himself in for. The director was relatively 'new to the game' and had previously had three non-executive appointments over a period of some two years. These had been in relatively straightforward circumstances (a new start, a management buy-out, and a re-investment) and the course they had run had also been relatively straightforward even if not always entirely predictable. The case described here, however, cannot remotely be described as either straightforward or predictable.

The company in question manufactured heavy fittings for the oil and gas and power generating industries. It had been established during the 1980s by three people from a company in a similar field who reckoned they could do it better: one of them was an extremely clever metallurgist who had worked out how to forge steels into shapes in such a way as not to compromise the metallurgical properties of the steel, thus preserving its strength at its weakest points, that is, on the bends. They had acquired a 'managing director' in the form of a local individual claiming to be a kind of freelance manager, who had participated in the original investment; they also appointed at the same time a non-executive chairman. The latter was himself the managing director of another company almost 300 miles away (though he was originally from the local area) and was believed to be, if not one of the great and the good, at least medium-sized and not bad.

After a couple of years of trading the directors had realized they needed increased working capital, and had gone with a proposal and a business plan to their local office of 3i. It had seemed like a decent prospect, and 3i had invested; although they had taken the right to nominate a non-exec, they had not yet done so because there was already the non-executive chairman there. But before long the company ran into some difficulties, and 3i became slightly concerned at the apparent lack of meaningful financial information emanating from it, so they exercised their right (with the full acquiescence of the existing board) and appointed J. as an additional non-executive director 'just to be sure that everything was all right'.

It fairly quickly became clear to J. that everything was in fact very far from being all right. Nothing ever seemed to be delivered on schedule, there were no procedures for order control, production control, financial control – nothing. The managing director was clearly not of the required calibre – it was unclear exactly what his supposed management experience consisted of, but it certainly wasn't much in evidence here. The chairman was an affable sort of person but totally ineffectual, achieving nothing during his one day per month on site. However, what was more worrying was that, try as he might, J. could not get some of the numbers to add up. There was a period of two months when no management accounts appeared – the chairman told J. not to worry, because it was the year-end and they would be overtaken anyway by the audited figures. One day J. was shown what purported to be a 'rough' management profit and loss statement for the December (the last month of the company's trading year) – it was handwritten, and didn't make any kind of sense in relation to the last figures which had been produced, for the October. Moreover, the accounts clerk herself confided to J. that she was not happy with the statement.

J. was now faced with a question: was this incompetence or something more serious? It appeared to him that there was almost too much that was wrong for it to be simply a matter of incompetence. It might have started out as that, but J. became increasingly concerned that something might be 'going on' – chiefly because of apparently unreconciled and unreconcilable raw material stock numbers. He reported to the 3i controller that he suspected the managing director could be up to no good, though it didn't seem there was any concrete proof. Some raw material stock items were being stored in the MD's yard at home, however, because there wasn't sufficient space at the factory, and some people suspected he might be selling off various bits and pieces for cash. Whatever the fact was, there was certainly a major discrepancy in the numbers. However, before anything could be proved, J. got a panic phone call one morning from the other directors saying the bank was about to pull the plug and could he do anything to help? The overdraft was up at nearly twice its nominal limit, and everyone in the company was more or less at their wits' end.

J. went in and discussed things with the other directors that afternoon, and almost before he knew it he was involved in a full-scale rescue operation. The managing director was summarily dismissed, as was the chairman shortly after, and the remaining directors persuaded the company's bank to give them three days in which to put together a recovery plan. They sold the plan to 3i, and prepared a presentation which was put to the bank at a meeting on the fourth day (at which the 3i controller was present and gave his moral support). The bank manager said 'that was the kind of presentation we ought to have had several months ago' (which rather begged the question of why they had allowed things to go on for so long, but it was hardly the occasion for debating niceties like that...) and the company secured its lifeline in the form of a temporary extension to the bank facility and additional equity from 3i, to be matched by additional investment from the directors. J. offered to participate in the additional investment, after first clearing the idea with the 3i controller, who thought it would be appropriate and would give the right sort of message both to the bank and to the other directors. His offer was accepted by the other directors.

It was agreed that J. should become executive chairman on a part-time basis, three days per week. Fortunately, he was able to reshuffle his other commitments in order to accommodate this new requirement, for which it was agreed at the outset that he should be paid 60 per cent of the pay of the highest-paid director, which seemed fair to everyone. They then embarked on a nail-biting attempt to turn the company round – it was effectively insolvent, but there was a clear and ongoing demand for its products and its customers did not seem to be unduly deterred by the changes in management and the obvious fact that it was struggling. There was, despite the antics of the previous MD, a reasonable volume of raw material stock, so there were unlikely to be massive supplier bills in the immediate term; provided they could get orders out more or less on time there was at least a fighting chance the company could survive. It was of course important to take all these factors into consideration, because it would have been quite wrong to carry on without such a fighting chance. In circumstances such as these, it is vitally necessary to be *seen* to be acting in good faith, so each board minute recorded that in the opinion of the directors the company would be able to meet its liabilities as and when they fell due – which, thanks to some leniency on the part of suppliers, was in fact the case. Even so, it was touch-and-go at times in the first few weeks, and in one of his reports J. identified what he described as 'a big requirement for brown trousers'!

There was also a need for some imaginative thinking. For example, there was one week when there was insufficient cash available to pay the wages. The company was hard up against its overdraft limit, and had to get the work out of the door in order to generate cash, but it isn't realistic to expect people to work for nothing. However, being a machining operation there was a lot of swarf created, so the workforce were issued with brooms and swept it all up, and the directors then did a cash job with a local scrap metal dealer and paid the wages in cash. Not quite, strictly speaking, within the letter of the law, but in the circumstances it was reckoned that the end justified the means, and indeed in due course events proved this to be right.

In terms of J.'s new role, it was a case of first of all identifying priorities. Clearly, financial stability was paramount. As it happened, they had been interviewing for the post of financial director just before the crisis broke, and had in fact offered the job to a candidate, who had accepted. Suddenly this poor guy must have wondered what on earth he was letting himself in for – his first task was to prepare at extremely short notice some financial projections to help to determine whether or not his new employers could survive, and then help to present these to the bank manager! Some baptism for him – it was probably fortunate for the company that he had burnt his boats with his previous post and so decided in spite of everything to stick with his new job. In the event he also turned out to be extremely competent and cool-headed, so it was clear from a very early stage that proper control was going to be established and maintained in that area.

The next priority was production control: sales were not a problem, but would soon become one if the company continued to let down its customers over delivery times. As it happened, J.'s basic management training, back in the late 1960s, had included substantial experience in work study and the associated management control systems. Since then he had found that this had frequently stood him in good stead, and nowhere was that more true than here. Even without detailed analysis, it was possible to put together some rudimentary process times and thereby to arrive at production cycle times and hence a rough schedule. 'You can't do it,' said the production people, 'every job is different'. But of course it could be done, and to give them their due, once they saw that it was possible to make up some form of schedule the production people took the task on, and over a period of time developed the whole process into something much more sophisticated, so that in reality all J. had to do was to act as a catalyst. Letting customers down over delivery times is less painful if you can give them a revised timetable *and then adhere to it*, and that is what J. and his colleagues managed to do, thus preserving the odd shred of credibility and doing much to safeguard further business.

On a slightly less intensely hands-on level, J. also played an important role in establishing standards in terms of how the place was managed and how customers and suppliers were treated, as well as in terms of how relations with the bank and the institutional investor were handled. In common with so many newish businesses, the company had not yet passed out of the 'entrepreneurial' mode into the 'managed' mode, and the way it conducted its operations reflected that. Its image was very much that of the 'oily-handed engineer', which J. worked hard to change into something rather more professional. It is worth making the point that they received excellent support throughout from both 3i and the National Westminster Bank.

One of the early problems the board was faced with boiled down to one of presentation. The company's financial year-end was 31 December, and as work on the audit for the year just past progressed it was clear that the published figures would be absolutely dreadful. As they were trying to rebuild supplier and customer confidence, it wasn't going to be helpful to have a set of figures showing a loss of over £400K and a company pretty well bust. On the assumption that the turnround was going to be successful, J. got agreement to a change in the year-end to 31 August: he reckoned that if they got the next audit for the eight-month period done quickly they would in fact be able to publish both sets of figures more or less together, which would show the turnround and hopefully give confidence in the management team. That is what they did, and it did have the desired effect. It is a card worth playing, in appropriate circumstances.

It took the best part of a year, but eventually the company emerged into profitability, where it remained throughout J.'s time there. It was the only manufacturer of its kind in the UK, and as such had several blue-chip clients such as Shell, Amoco, Elf, Babcock, and the Weir group, and there is little doubt that such a client list helped its overall credibility and strengthened the 'professional' image referred to above. There remained a tendency to fly somewhat by the seat of the pants, but because product quality was maintained and because the technical people clearly knew what they were talking about, the perception in the market place was in general reasonably favourable.

Once the business was on a sound footing, a new managing director was recruited and J. reverted to being non-executive chairman, with time to look at the more 'traditional' types of things such as remuneration surveys, company cars and setting up a company pension plan. Actually, this latter wasn't as straightforward as might be supposed, for one of the directors was a Jehovah's Witness. Armageddon was on the horizon (at that time it was believed to be due around the turn of the millennium, though that estimate was subsequently revised in the light of experience) and so he didn't see any point in setting up a pension scheme for people who wouldn't be around to collect a pension! However, he was persuaded that there might be the opportunity for some of the company's employees to collect at least part of their entitlement before the end of the world as mankind knew it, so a scheme was duly established.

Finally, some eight years after his original appointment, J. came off the board after helping to recruit his successor as non-executive chairman.

This case is a good illustration of the thesis on which this book is based. J. was originally appointed as the investing institution's nominee, partly to be their eyes and ears but partly also out of a genuine feeling that the board needed strengthening. The other directors did not, in this case, suspect any ulterior motive, which actually said a great deal for the way in which 3i (and more particularly the individual investment controller in the case) handled J.'s appointment. His remit, of course, changed dramatically when things went wrong, but it was interesting that *he* was the person the other directors turned to – 'we need help; *you'll* have to help us'. It simply would not have been of any use to them if J. had stood off and said in effect 'sorry guys, I'm a non-exec, you'll have to get yourselves a new leader somewhere else' because there wasn't time to do that – if you have three days in which to put together a rescue plan you get on with it, and what is more, if you are one of the people who are seeking the confidence and the backing of the financiers then there is no way that you can simply drop out once that backing has been obtained. You are part of the solution, and if you aren't prepared to get involved to that extent you shouldn't be there.

For a while, J. was the leader, and without doubt had to display the kinds of competencies related to that role. It wasn't really appropriate for him to have an especially close relationship with any individual director as a mentor or confidant, but he certainly was a thinker, a doer, an evaluator, a networker, and a terminator – and, it could be argued, a mole, although the relationship with the institution was for most of this period a strong and relatively mutually trusting one so that there wasn't the element of suspicion that tends to accompany a mole. In terms of the competencies required, J. needed all of the distinguishing competencies at one time or another, plus most of the threshold ones as well.

The company was certainly still in the childhood stage when J. joined it. During his time there, it did mature noticeably, beginning to show signs of stability in some of its systems, and although it could not realistically be said to have reached maturity by the time he left (and, given the high degree of individuality of many of its senior people, perhaps it was destined never to fully mature) it had definitely progressed to the mature end of the adolescence category.

There is no doubt that J. had to get his hands dirty (at times, literally so) and he needed to show both personal and financial commitment – it was fortunate, therefore, that he was in a position to be able to do so, and that he was able to drop other things he was involved in so as to give himself the necessary scope. Had this not been the case, there would be a serious question as to the value of a non-exec in those circumstances. J. was clearly in a position where he was able to add value, and later, when he was no longer adding value, he ceased to be a director. The experience was, in sum, highly beneficial to both parties: J's reputation and 'marketability' were enhanced, and a business was built which in the event proved to be sufficiently strong to withstand the vagaries of its sector over the last fifteen years and is still trading today.

Summary of key points

Stage of company's evolution:	Childhood, approaching adolescence
Role/s played by non-exec:	Leader
	Thinker
	Doer
	Evaluator
	Networker
	Terminator
	Mole
Competencies required:	**Thinking** – all
	Getting results – Initiative
	– Results focus
	– Thoroughness
	– Determination
	– Critical information seeking
	– Concern for standards

Influencing	- Interpersonal awareness
	- Persuasiveness
	- Organizational awareness
	- Strategic influencing
Self-managing	- Self-control
	- Independence
	- Self-development
	- Positive self-image
	- Flexibility

7

Headwear and Neckwear Manufacturer

Very occasionally, success arises from the ashes of failure. More often, one failure simply breeds another. This particular case came into the latter category, though it very nearly came into the former.

The company had started life as a resurrection from the remains of a group of companies which had themselves been part of a by then-defunct conglomerate, typical of the kind that had sprung up during the 1980s. It manufactured items for a range of retail outlets including Marks & Spencer. Interestingly, two rival teams had approached a venture capital provider for backing to set up the venture, each going to a different office of the provider! The team that had gone to the office nearest to where the company was located turned out to be the successful one. They set off with great gusto and a board of directors that was essentially dysfunctional – the managing director was not up to the job; he and the sales director couldn't stand one another; the finance director, though very competent, was relatively inexperienced and was so young that some, including the managing director, didn't take him seriously; there was no production director, so that a manufacturing organization had no manufacturing representation on the board; and the managing director's brother (who was little more than a stores clerk) was also on the board. Not, it might be thought, an ideal recipe for a successful venture, and it does appear a legitimate cause for wonder why the institutional investor did not insist that a non-exec be put on the board right at the start.

The key point to understand about this situation is that this was in the days when M & S still prided themselves on using exclusively UK suppliers, and they were tough on those suppliers. As far as M & S was concerned, one receivership at a supplier's was one too many, so the 'phoenix' company was in effect always at a disadvantage, trying from its very first day to retrieve a situation it had inherited. Even had it had a thoroughly competent team at the helm, it would have struggled, particularly in its early weeks and months. By the time the venture capital investment controller nominated R. to the board, some four months after the start-up, things were not looking too good – the board was clearly not in control of the situation, and it was made clear to R. that his role was to try to get things back on track.

From the very start, this was not an easy task for R. Because of the tensions within the board, and more widely in the senior management team, it was difficult to establish exactly what was happening and who were the goodies and who the baddies. R. had to rely to a very large extent on information given to him, and of course at first he had no way of knowing whose information was reliable and whose wasn't – what was clear, however, was that unless someone started laying down the law the company was going nowhere. To start with, R. took the view that it had to be up to the MD to lay down the law. He, after all, was the man in charge, and it was he whom the investing institution had backed. However, the extent of the pressures, both within the company and outside, soon persuaded R. that this individual was not a particularly good bet.

But the fact was that, despite everything, he was the one whom the institution had backed, so there must have been at some time a perception that he was 'backable'. Consequently, if that judgement was to be challenged it was important for R. to get things right and make sure as far as possible that his own judgement was sound. So R. began by confiding in the investment controller that he couldn't really see the MD being a successful leader in the long run. This was accepted, but the view was that, for the present at least, there wasn't a realistic alternative – and R. had, however reluctantly, to accept that view. There were some quite competent people at middle management level, and so the game plan had to be to try to achieve as much as possible through them in the short term and perhaps lessen the influence of the MD. That, then, became R's remit: one that wasn't particularly easy on the basis of a non-executive presence.

Matters were not helped by an unsympathetic bank. Curiously, when the original deal had been done, rather than set the project up in the first place with a facility at a High Street lender, the team had opted to go with a well-known merchant bank. It is extremely unlikely that the reasons for this had much to do with any real potential benefit that might be derived, and in fact it is almost certain that the overall situation would have been better if the original deal had been set up with the involvement of a High Street lender, for despite any reservations one may have about levels of competence and understanding in banks, few would probably argue with the contention that a merchant bank is even less likely than a High Street lender to relate to a small business. Nevertheless, whatever the rights and wrongs, they were with a merchant bank, and the bank was getting somewhat nervous and somewhat heavy.

However, after some initial work R. was able to go off as he had originally planned for two weeks' summer holiday, leaving matters stable although not brilliant. He came back to almost complete chaos. The factory holiday had started and the MD had gone away; during his absence all sorts of things had come to light about poor decisions and management failures. The finance director showed R. some projections which suggested that the company would go bust within a matter almost of days, and the sales director was tearing his hair at the interference he had suffered from the MD while trying to re-establish the company's credibility with its major customers. R. was asked to attend a meeting with a financial consultant at which it became clear that a crisis was only hours away and that only by radical action could matters be put right. So after a first day back from holiday of almost 24 hours of non-stop meetings, R. found himself becoming part of an attempt to bring the company round.

The venture capitalists were informed, and after much discussion agreed that it seemed most unlikely that the MD was worth retaining. The particular investment controller was not the world's best at personal relations, and neither the sales director nor the finance director found it easy to relate to him, so R. needed to work very hard to keep everyone working in harmony. It was agreed that the MD should be got rid of, though the two other senior directors were less willing than R. was for it to be done in a civilized manner. This was due partly to the financial state of the company – there was no way they could afford to pay out any settlement package, and in any case the other directors didn't see why the person they considered responsible for the present dire state of affairs should be handed money when the company was having obvious difficulty in paying suppliers whose goodwill was much more essential to the company's future. R. had some sympathy for that point of view, but argued that didn't necessarily make it right for them to rub the MD's nose in the dirt – he had, after all, not been indulging in any illegal or unethical activities, but had simply not been up to the job.

So, the day he returned from holiday, R. went into the MD's office to see him, prepared for perhaps a lengthy termination negotiation. R. started by saying 'we have a problem', and the MD rather astonished him by replying 'yes, I understand that. I think I should go.' As so often is the case, he knew perfectly well what the situation was and was under no illusions about his own position. His only concern was that he should be allowed to go with his dignity intact, and at that point R. saw no reason to deny him that. It was made clear to him that the company could not afford anything in the way of a severance package at that stage, so it was suggested that he resigned voluntarily, and R. gave an undertaking that if cash flow permitted they would try to pay his salary for three months. He held, of course, a large equity stake in the company, but it was agreed that should not be treated as an issue at this stage. When he had gone, R. took pains to make it clear to the MD's brother that his own position was not in itself affected by the MD's departure. Although it was pretty clear that the brother was not contributing much to the company's wellbeing, it would have been quite wrong (and could have led to legal action) to link his position to the MD's, so he was told that his future depended entirely on his own performance. He was, however, voted off the board straight away.

Unlike a lot of small businesses, this company was unionized, so it was particularly important to be seen to be communicating properly. Indeed, the first thing R. did after the MD had driven away (in his company car which he was told he could keep for a limited period) was to get all the workers and staff together to tell them what was going on. They weren't given any false hopes, but of course it was necessary to put a reasonably positive 'spin' on things otherwise there was a risk of losing staff at a time when the company needed all the help and support they could give. This was in fact the first of many such 'mass meetings', and marked a change in the company's culture which most seemed to appreciate.

So a new regime and a new management style were inaugurated, and for a while things seemed to go the company's way. The first major hurdle was the negotiation of the hoped-for next contract with Marks & Spencer, and R. went to London to lend moral support to the sales director at a Baker Street meeting. M & S were persuaded that the company was still a credible supplier, and shortly afterwards the second-largest customer also declared their continuing support and promised large volumes of new season business. Cash was, not surprisingly, very tight, but the finance director proved to have the necessary juggling skills. (He still didn't much like R's idea of behaving in a civilized manner towards the ex-MD, and when it came down to it R. actually found it increasingly difficult to argue with him when it came to a toss-up between keeping suppliers happy and paying salary to the ex-MD.) R. carried out a fairly quick appraisal of the key members of staff: one or two, including the ex-MD's brother, were got rid of, and a few others were given good reasons not to stay.

Working capital, as so often seems to be the case, was the principal problem the team faced. Although the finance director got the short-term position under control, it was clear that there was a potential inadequacy over the coming twelve months, and a re-financing was going to be necessary. For reasons which were never in fact made clear, the venture capital investors were equivocal about this. Maybe it was a case of 'once bitten...' but, whatever the thinking, the attitude of the particular investment controller seemed to be that he would rather be somewhere else. Rather grudgingly, he eventually agreed that his institution would consider investing if other sources of additional capital could be found. So it turned into a race against time, with the bank now making it clear that its support would continue only for a limited period. A possible capital restructuring was worked out, but this depended on the ex-MD agreeing to a significant loss on his original stake. He indicated that he wasn't prepared to accept this – notwithstanding the obvious fact that it was largely a result of his inadequacy that the situation had arisen. With this unresolved problem, no other potential investor would look at the company, and so R. and his team had to try instead for a trade sale.

Almost immediately, they received an expression of interest. The 'losing' buy-out team from the phoenix days the previous summer had thrown in their lot with a London-based specialist clothing manufacturer and set up a subsidiary operation only about ten miles from where R. was attempting his rescue operation. The London parent asked to meet R, and matters quickly moved to a negotiating situation. They brought up their advisers, to whose attitude R. took a major dislike (though he was very careful not to show this) – they clearly regarded R. and his colleagues as country bumpkins from out in the sticks. *They* were men of the world, *they* knew about things like take-overs, and the local team was treated with a degree of disdain. After a while, they decided that, rather than take on the company as a going concern, it would be more clever to buy the business from a receiver. R. pointed out that this would be self-defeating: Marks & Spencer would be extremely unlikely to tolerate a second receivership within a period of less than a year. However, his arguments were to no avail – *they* knew better! The investment controller had by now become virtually invisible, so R. had nowhere really to turn to and the bank seemed almost glad to contemplate a receivership. So it duly happened, and the London company bought the business from the receiver. As expected, almost the first thing that then happened was that Marks & Spencer cancelled their new season's order, and the new company itself went into receivership a few months later.

Almost certainly, a spot of *schadenfreude* might have been forgivable. The main feeling on the part of R. and his team, however, was one of frustration, because in fact the whole thing so nearly succeeded. Looking back afterwards, R. genuinely could not think of anything he could or should have done differently, except perhaps to have moved against the MD earlier – but he felt he had no real justification for doing so on the basis of the information available to him at the time. As a non-exec you are to a large extent dependent on the information you are given, and you may not have any control over the quality of that information. This is of course particularly important if your main source of information happens to be a major part of the problem. Had this been a bigger company, it seems probable that R. could have obtained better information sooner, and perhaps had a little longer to work out the best course of action, but as it was it was a case of 'panic stations', he had to take control and do something quickly.

It is also interesting to reflect, once again, that when the other directors perceived the wheels as being about to fall off, they came to their non-exec. They said '*you* must help us, *you* must do this, do that, do the other' – executive or non-executive simply didn't enter into it, it was a matter of who was regarded as the best person to take a lead. In such a situation, R. would have been useless if he had opted to be in stand-off mode.

Very much the same range of roles and competencies came into evidence here as with the first case study. Yet, in the end, it was a failure, so does that undermine the author's theory in relation to non-executive appointments? Probably not: in fact, it leaves it relatively intact, because the rescue was so nearly successful. In the end, the most likely explanation for what killed this company was people, and relationships between people. The board as originally constituted was incapable of functioning effectively, there wasn't the right chemistry between the directors and the venture capital investment controller, the banking set-up was all wrong, and at the end the would-be trade purchasers were fundamentally out of sympathy with the local people and conditions. If R. had been appointed sooner – especially perhaps if he had been there from the very start – things might have been different. For one thing, it is likely that under those circumstances the banking arrangements would have been different, and for another thing R. might have been able to prevent the board from becoming quite so dysfunctional. Perhaps, though, R. shouldn't have gone in in the first place – indeed, one accountant with whom he discussed the case some years later said, a bit stuffily, 'well, of course, you should have done your own due diligence before agreeing to go in'. That is typical accountantspeak, the voice of clean hands! It is of course true, in an ideal world, but the world of SMEs is rarely ideal and if you are to make any impact you have to be prepared to take a chance. In doing so, the dividing line between success and failure can be incredibly thin.

Interestingly, in many respects this company was quite mature, despite its obvious problems. It had of course had a previous existence, as part of the large group which had gone down, so its systems and procedures were relatively sound, and at no time did R. need to lead anyone by the nose through a learning process. The weakness of the management set-up was the Achilles heel: it compromised the emotional atmosphere to the extent that the company appeared to be going through a kind of second childhood, and R. found it intensely frustrating at times when senior managers failed or refused to show the breadth of vision that was necessary. Even allowing for that, however, with a better financial position which could have provided a bit of breathing space for the necessary management changes to take proper effect, the balance of probability has always seemed to R. that the company itself could have survived and regained its maturity.

Summary of key points

Stage of company's evolution:	Maturity, but elements of childishness	
Role/s played by non-exec:	Leader	
	Thinker	
	Doer	
	Evaluator	
	Networker	
	Terminator	
	Mole	
Competencies required:	**Thinking**	- all
	Getting results	- Initiative
		- Results focus
		- Thoroughness
		- Determination
		- Critical information seeking
		- Concern for standards

Influencing	- Interpersonal awareness
	- Concern for impact
	- Persuasiveness
	- Organizational awareness
	- Strategic influencing
	- Situational sensitivity
Self-managing	- Self-control
	- Independence
	- Self-development
	- Positive self-image
	- Flexibility

8
Computer and Office Supplies Catalogue Company

This was in some respects a sad case, but it did nonetheless bring its own satisfaction to the non-exec, albeit of a sober kind. It also illustrates well, once again, the point so frequently made throughout this book about the need to be prepared to act in a 'hands-on' capacity when circumstances demand and people turn to you.

The company was a catalogue sales operation dealing in computer-related items and other office supplies, and had been set up with funding from Scottish Enterprise, 3i, and James Findlay Bank. At the time T. was introduced, it was into its second year, but had in its first year failed to get anywhere near its projected sales volume. Naturally, an operation like this relies on guaranteed availability and speedy turnround of items, so extensive stock has to be carried; in the case of this company, someone had either seriously underestimated the cost burden of the initial stocking or been hopelessly optimistic in forecasting sales – it was difficult to tell which, but the first year's result was a loss equivalent to the year's total turnover.

There had been a non-executive chairman right from the start: a working executive in another company, and a competent person in his own right. He was quite good at the straightforward 'procedural' side of being a chairman – chairing meetings and so on – but didn't appear to have a great deal apart from that to bring to the party. It was difficult to avoid the impression that he was somewhat out of his depth in the situation that had developed. T. was nominated by 3i and Scottish Enterprise jointly, who had by now lost confidence in the ability of the existing board to deal with things. Curiously, when he attended his first board meeting, he found that the relevant investment controllers from all three institutional investors were accustomed also to attend each meeting, something he had not come across before (and, indeed, something the author has not come across anywhere else, either). T. took this, too, as tantamount to an oblique expression of lack of confidence in the board as constituted.

The managing director was totally committed and, in fact, quite competent. Indeed, much the same could be said for all the company's employees, several of whom (not just the directors) had invested their own money in the start-up. The problem was that nobody had foreseen such a poor first year's performance, and it was so far adrift of their expectations that nobody had much of a clue how to cope. They were, in effect, more or less in a state of shock. To add to the problems, the managing director's health was somewhat suspect: he had just completed a course of treatment for throat cancer, on top of which a member of his immediate family apparently had a worrying health problem. So he was under a degree of stress that is difficult to imagine, and it surely spoke volumes for his tremendous strength of character that he continued to give 100 per cent and more to the business.

The basic problem, of course, was underfunding – nothing unusual there, then. Whoever it was who had done the original projections certainly hadn't done the management team any favours. One of the things T. learned very quickly was that it is a fact of life in the catalogue sales business that your best (and maybe only) chance of good sales levels is to produce regular updates of your catalogue and to send them out to ever-expanding mailing lists. Both of these cost money, on top of the cost already referred to of setting up and maintaining the required stock levels. Each successive edition of your catalogue has to look like a new edition, not just a reprint of an increasingly tired original, so there also has to be an element of design input, quite apart from the obvious set-up and print costs. Mailing lists have to be bought, and although these are in fact fairly readily available they can cost a substantial amount when you're talking about the size of list needed for a viable catalogue distribution. If you haven't enough money to do all this, you can quickly go into a downward spiral. The catalogue goes to the same mailing list each time and the recipients may not actually want to make further purchases just now; if it doesn't change it is considered tired and out-of-date, so not much is sold from it, and this makes it hard to afford to produce and circulate a new one, so it gets more tired and out-of-date, and so on.

The reaction to T.'s appointment was mixed. The MD was pleased: he saw T. as a support and a confidant, and certainly not as a mole, a hit-man, or anything in the least sinister. Apart from his own problems, he gave the impression of finding life very lonely – as so many MDs do – and to have someone around who was actively supportive and non-judgemental seemed, in fact, to be good for him. He and T. quickly established a good *rapport*. Some of the other members of the team were a little less welcoming, feeling perhaps under threat and therefore perceiving T.'s appointment as a concrete manifestation of the lack of investor confidence: in particular, he got slightly negative vibrations from the finance director, who probably felt especially vulnerable to criticism. However, T. worked hard to try to dispel any perception that he was there to bear down on anyone, because it was clearly important that all the staff regained some measure of confidence in themselves and their company, and on the whole he was able to form good relations with everyone. As he wasn't there on any executive basis, to lead a rescue, there was no question of usurping anyone's authority, which almost certainly helped the relationships to be smoother.

Of course, everyone was anxious to do everything possible to save the company, and short-term cost savings were identified in terms of salary sacrifices and related items. Over a period of some three months or so, they were able to produce two new editions of the catalogue, and each time there was an immediate boost in sales. It was, however, clear to everyone involved that this kind of programme was sustainable only for a short time: they calculated the sums that would be needed to enable the company to operate as it really should do, expanding its catalogue and producing a fresh edition at intervals of not more than two months (and ideally less than that), and buying new mailing lists regularly, and none of the institutional investors was prepared to pledge the requisite amount. Meanwhile, T. was reassuring the managing director as far as he could that his nagging sore throat was most probably not a recurrence of his cancer but just a stress-related symptom.

Of the institutional investors, only 3i and their representative investment controller seemed switched on to commercial reality – the others confined their input largely to hand-wringing. The 3i controller and T. worked quite closely together; they eventually concluded that a trade sale might be possible and should be pursued as the only option other than a liquidation. There were at that time two major UK catalogue companies in this sector, but it appeared that neither of them was in a position just then to be interested. However, quite by chance a major American player happened to be looking at the possibility of setting up in the UK, so they were approached with the suggestion that an acquisition might be an easier means of entry than a totally new start. Their Chief Executive was persuaded to come to over London, and T. and the MD went to meet him there to see what kind of a deal could be done. They did not really have any high cards.

Fortunately, however, the American CEO recognized the benefits he could get in the short term from a ready-made product list, a management team, and a network, and he decided to buy. Perhaps 'buy' is a bit of an over-statement – in fact, he paid £1 and took on the bank debt, which in the circumstances was about the best that could be expected from the company's point of view. The institutions got nothing, and likewise all the individual members of staff who had sunk their cash into the venture lost it all. But the staff all got jobs under the new ownership, and they and the institutions were spared the trauma of a liquidation, emerging with some dignity, if nothing else. Afterwards, T. was thanked by the 3i controller for his efforts: it is perhaps worth noting that this does not happen all that often (in fact, it was one of only two occasions that T. experienced it, and other institutionally-appointed non-execs seem to return similar statistics). The company became quite successful under its new ownership, though lack of time prevented T. from keeping in touch, and it is not known for how long any of the original team remained there.

So what are the implications of this case? It could be argued that the enterprise was a very sick child which was in fact already doomed by the time T. was appointed, and that to seek any lessons you have to go right back to its formation – for example, should T. (or indeed anyone) have accepted a non-executive appointment in a company which was so woefully under-financed and which therefore had little chance of survival? It is an interesting question with perhaps no obvious answer, but it is legitimate to argue that the original non-executive chairman could reasonably have expected a group of three institutions such as 3i, Scottish Enterprise, and James Findlay Bank to have done their homework sufficiently thoroughly for the venture to be backable. What did become very clear was that, when the wheels began to fall off, although there was no obvious incompetence among the management, there was nevertheless no-one with the strength or ability to push through the measures that were needed or to generate the necessary energy and confidence. Perhaps, then, at that stage, the chairman should have resigned, willingly or otherwise, to make way for someone like T. who could have provided the required input: certainly he played no part in the efforts to save the business, and it is difficult to envisage that he would have had much of a profile in the kind of competency analysis described in Chapter 3. The probability is that, had T. not been appointed, the company would have drifted fairly quickly into liquidation, so overall the moral must once again be that non-involvement is no use when a company hits problems.

From the point of view of what T. did, and what his involvement was, clearly his direct involvement was less than in either of the two previous examples in this section of the book. At no time was it suggested that he should take an executive role, and neither did he become chairman – whether this in fact had a bearing on how effective he was able to be is difficult to say, but it must be a possibility that by the time of his appointment the damage had been so great as to be, in effect, most probably irreparable. A refinancing *might* perhaps have been a realistic prospect if the company had been perceived as having strong enough leadership, which T. *might* have been able to provide if he'd been asked, but with hindsight there is not really a convincing case that this option would have been viable. However, one thing that was important was that T. did not shirk any involvement. He became thoroughly engaged in the company's struggle for survival, and was clearly identified by both staff and investors as part of that struggle; hence he was in a position to bring influence to the strategy, as well as doing what he could to support and maintain the self-image of those involved by, among other things, projecting on his own behalf a thoroughly positive self-image.

T.'s main roles were those of mentor and confidant (to the MD), thinker and networker. Sadly, all this was not enough to secure for the company a future as an independent entity, but all the evidence suggests that, in all probability, without his having been there the company would not have survived as long as it did, there would have been a liquidation and no future at all for anyone. It was a sobering experience for all concerned, one which helps to illustrate how inexorable a downward path can be, but at the same time how something can at times be salvaged if everybody has the will for that to happen. A non-exec isn't meant to be a miracle-worker, but he may have the capacity, and the opportunity, to make a situation less dire than it might otherwise be. That, in the end, was perhaps what T. managed to achieved here – as such, it does represent success of a sort, notwithstanding the eventual outcome.

Summary of key points

Stage of company's evolution:　Infancy-childhood

Role/s played by non-exec:　Mentor
　　　　　　　　　　　　　　　Confidant
　　　　　　　　　　　　　　　Thinker
　　　　　　　　　　　　　　　Networker

Competencies required:	Thinking	- all
	Getting results	- Initiative
		- Results focus
		- Thoroughness
		- Determination
		- Critical information seeking
		- Concern for efficiency
	Influencing	- Interpersonal awareness
		- Persuasiveness
		- Organizational awareness
		- Strategic influencing
		- Relationship building
		- Situational sensitivity
	Self-managing	- Self-control
		- Independence
		- Self-development
		- Positive self-image
		- Flexibility

9
Professional Services Company

This was an appointment which ran for the appointee the whole gamut between success and failure, elation and despair.

It started (as so many do) with an approach from a local office of an investing institution. They had some years previously financed a management buy-out in the particular company, a locally well-known professional services provider. Their investment had been at a reasonably significant level, but they hadn't appointed a nominee to the board because there was already a non-executive chairman in post. However, the day came when he indicated his desire to move on, and as it happened this coincided with a difficult period for the company, so the brief being discussed for any successor was more than just a watching one and the appointment was termed a 'semi-executive' directorship! The institution had identified S. and another individual as potential candidates, leaving it to the company itself to make the choice.

The company had in fact been in existence for over twenty years, but in its present form only since the buy-out from the original organization some five years earlier. The actual buy-out team had comprised several individuals, but by the time of S.'s appointment only one of these was still around: he was managing director and held nearly 50 per cent of the equity. The company had achieved some good results for the first couple of years following the buy-out but had then declined, and in the year immediately prior to S.'s appointment had had a fairly spectacularly bad result with a loss of over £200K. There was at the same time a major falling-out among senior management and most of the other directors left, three of them subsequently setting up their own rival company.

On the face of it, there was nothing particularly remarkable about this. In the professional services sector, there tends to be quite a lot of coming and going – partly perhaps because a fairly typical pattern is for young people to join the business, become trained, and then find insufficient career prospects and so move to more senior positions in other companies within the sector or, indeed, set up their own companies; perhaps also partly because these businesses are by their very nature extremely people-centered, and any strains and tensions will tend to become exacerbated by the closeness of the working relationships and so can lead all the sooner to break-ups.

However, this company did give the impression of being perhaps a peculiarly extreme case of falling out, and quite apart from the impact of the other directors' departures it did seem that something must be seriously wrong within the organization for such a poor result to have been achieved for the year just ended. There was a suggestion that all was not well internally in HR terms, and to an extent this was confirmed by the managing director himself when S. went to meet him for the first time to discuss the possibility of his appointment. S. had bumped into him once or twice previously on the local business 'circuit' and had formed the opinion that although clearly competent in his own field he was most probably not the easiest of people to have a close relationship with. The two of them, however, hit it off remarkably well on the occasion of their first discussion, and the MD was refreshingly honest about what he saw as his own shortcomings on the HR side. He was full of ideas about the further development of the business, and admitted that he was looking for a fairly high degree of hands-on involvement – he wasn't in the least unhappy about the 'semi-executive' nature of S.'s proposed appointment. Quite the reverse, in fact: he had a ready-made wish list of things he wanted the new appointee (whoever that might be) to major in.

S. met the other directors as well (or, at least, the two that were left following the mass exodus a few months previously, though S. didn't meet the non-executive chairman) and formed the opinion that they were somewhat in the MD's shadow but, possibly, content to be there for the time being. What S. found especially interesting about this whole process was that it was the first time in his non-executive life that he had actually gone through anything approaching a formal selection procedure, involving meetings with all his prospective colleagues and an agreed remit most of which was written down.

In due course S. was selected and appointed, and set about fulfilling his role. To a large extent, this was at first almost project-based: many of the things the MD wanted to achieve were translatable into projects, and several of these involved different members of the staff, which was also valuable to S. because it gave him the opportunity to get to know the organization and many of the people in it. The MD said that he felt there was a need for a fundamental culture change, and S. had no doubt that he was right. The MD himself was by nature rather autocratic, but was highly intelligent and recognized his own nature. Moreover, he was well aware that there were times when an autocratic approach could be quite counterproductive: what he really wanted was for someone to create a more open and democratic environment which would help to achieve the development in the organization that he realized he could not bring about by himself. He and S. managed in the first few weeks and months to build a very good working relationship, and when the non-executive chairman left, four months after S. joined, S. became chairman, and the managing director–chairman axis worked most effectively.

With the MD's agreement (and active encouragement) S. got closely involved with the recruitment of new staff, particularly at senior levels, and he also conducted the termination interviews whenever anyone left – this also added to the insight he was gaining into the company's workings. In fact, the organization now began to stabilize noticeably: staff turnover had run almost out of control during the months prior to S.'s appointment, but by the end of that trading year, six months later, had slowed to a trickle. The year's result was a break-even, and at the AGM the managing director publicly paid S. the compliment of saying that he had done more than anyone to get the company back on an even keel, which was very generous of him and a testimony to the relationship established between them.

By now, the business was sufficiently stable for some thought to be given to the future beyond the next month's fees! The board and senior management were strengthened by new appointments, and in what turned out to be a stimulating and enjoyable process a five-year strategy was developed in which the board identified both market sectors and geographical areas into which they saw advantage in moving. A possible flotation was seen as the end of this strategy. A new divisional structure was created, with each division being given its own brand name and identity, and a more formalized approach to training was inaugurated – one of the newly-appointed directors was strong on training and development, and had considerable expertise in that area, and S. worked closely with this individual in implementing a whole new training system. At the same time, S. recognized that the old autocratic structure had meant there were very few people in the organization capable of taking on much in the way of increased responsibility; drawing on some of his own previous professional experience he put together a management development programme and worked through it by running training seminars for a group of people identified by the board as having the potential for promotion. One of the things that was new about the approach S. took was that he included in the group not only 'mainstream' consultants but also suitable people from the 'back office' administrative and accounting areas in the company.

Among the items on the managing director's 'wish list' was a proposed tie-up with a third party company, operating in another field which was however in some ways related to the field in which his company operated. He felt that there could be some synergy here: the networks into which his organization had an input might well be relevant and indeed valuable for individuals who were using the services of the third party company. The particular company he was courting was based at the opposite end of the country, but was anxious to expand its field of operations – it had on a previous occasion tried to enter the market in the region where the subject company operated but had not succeeded, so there was a strong incentive to succeed the second time round.

It was agreed that S. should take on the proposed tie-up as one of his projects, and accordingly he put in a great deal of time and effort during his second year with the company towards setting up a joint venture. Now, it is a fact of life that joint ventures are always potentially problematical: they can depend to a significant extent on inter-personal relationships, and if the chemistry isn't right they probably are doomed to failure. In this case, the chemistry between S.'s MD and the MD of the other company never really worked properly, so that although S. himself got on well enough with both of them he found himself increasingly in the role of not merely go-between but peacemaker, and fairly soon the interests of the two organizations threatened to come into conflict. S. was in fact a director both of the original company and of the joint venture, so his position became over a period of time somewhat difficult. To make matters worse, the actual business of the new joint venture didn't take off as well as had been hoped, with the result that the original company was faced with possible financial losses arising from the venture – losses which, after the experience of two years previously, did not do much for the local MD's equilibrium. The relationship between him and S. began for the first time to experience an element of tension, although at first this was not very pronounced, and did not for the time being get in the way of either of their roles.

At around the same time, it was decided that the company should take on a finance director, and S. interviewed the candidates along with the MD. In the event, they were agreed on the successful candidate: an extremely bright person, some fifteen years younger than the MD and

S., with a degree as well as his accountancy qualification. They both felt that he might be somewhat abrasive, but it seemed to both of them that this would be no bad thing, since the accounting side of the company had become rather sleepy and there was a clear need to match the new operational structure with a new structure of financial accountabilities. Again, neither the MD nor S. saw any harm in the possibility of some grit in a relationship, provided the fundamentals were right.

The new FD proved to be worth his weight in gold. The management accounts were sharpened up, the budgetary process suddenly became rigorous and meaningful, and relations between the company and its bankers were put on a new and much more professional footing. As the chairman and MD had foreseen, however, it was not long before some elements of tension began to develop between the FD and one or two of the other directors – he didn't suffer fools gladly, as expected, and in his opinion there were fools on the board. One in particular of the other directors was underperforming, and the FD made no secret of his opinion that the guy should be got rid of. This posed an interesting problem for S. Initially, his own view tended towards being content to leave the particular individual in place for a while longer – although by no means a star, he was not without ability, he had some subordinates who were performing effectively, and S. was concerned to maintain some stability, conscious of the previous problems and their impact on the company's results. However, the FD argued very strongly that, given the direction in which they were seeking to take the organization, they couldn't realistically afford highly-paid underperformers, and not only was this person underperforming as a manager but he was also manifestly not board material. On reflection, S. recognized that this was undeniably true; he became convinced that on balance the business would be stronger if the individual was not around, and that the deed should be done quickly. The MD became similarly convinced, and the director in question was persuaded to leave (with, however, a reasonable termination package). Faced with a need for an internal reorganization, the MD and S. then agreed that the FD was in fact the most obvious candidate for the job on account of his clear management capability. So the FD now took over a major part of the departed director's area of responsibility, relinquishing his day-to-day financial responsibilities when the company took on an accounts manager who it was considered had the potential to make it through to an FD's post in due course.

For a time, this worked well. The ex-FD was, as noted above, a strong manager and proved to be an excellent motivator of his staff, and the division's performance was good. The MD thought highly of him, despite the abrasiveness, and both of them worked hard at their relationship. Thus S. was chairing an increasingly strong board, and although he found himself being used from time to time by both the MD and the FD as a confidant and a sounding-board for their respective frustrations with each other, it seemed to him that the tensions were helping to build an overall team which was increasingly capable of taking the business to new heights – and this was borne out by the results the business was achieving.

It was difficult for S. to be sure exactly when things started to go wrong, or what triggered the deterioration. Probably it was a number of things, any of which by itself would have been a problem without necessarily being terminal, but which in combination proved unsustainable.

The director who was leading the internal training and development efforts had, for family reasons, to begin diminishing her role. Her domestic situation in fact worsened, and before long she had more or less to withdraw completely from any active participation in the company's activities. Much of the good work she had done was then largely undone by the MD, who rather suddenly and without warning reverted to his old autocratic stance and tried almost to reimpose the kind of HR regime which had existed in years gone by. In the light of his previous support for the 'reformist' policies that had been introduced, this was rather surprising and most disappointing, and not unnaturally led to major arguments with other senior people, especially the ex-FD. The MD had some problems of his own outside work, which created additional tensions at work and also made him somewhat paranoid about the company's short-term financial performance. It certainly seemed very much to S. that his altered behaviour was probably largely attributable to his personal problems.

But whatever the causes, the results of the changes the MD's colleagues saw in him were not long in coming, and when they did come they affected things right across the business. Relations between the company and the joint venture partner were soon deteriorating to an alarming degree, despite S.'s efforts. The ex-FD became increasingly intolerant of the MD's attitude, and a dispute arose between them over whether there should be a replacement FD: the MD wanted to recruit one, and was highly critical of the accounts manager's performance, whilst the ex-FD (supported by S.) felt that the accounts manager had what it took, and would make the grade being looked for within an acceptable period of time.

It seemed now to S. that there were ominous signs that history might be in danger of repeating itself. Acutely conscious of what the company had been through prior to his appointment, he began to be concerned at the MD's attitude and performance, and wondered about the individual's ability to take the company forward in line with the five-year strategy. He discussed his misgivings in detail with the institutional investor, and the local director pronounced himself satisfied with the five-year strategy and concluded that now he was, in effect, backing S. and the ex-FD rather than the MD. S., meanwhile, was becoming more and more convinced that the future of the company did not lie with the current MD, and the institution indicated that they shared his view.

It is important to be clear that this was not in any way meant to be a personal vendetta on S.'s part. His concern was to safeguard the company's future and that of its stakeholders, and if that meant that the biggest shareholder–director had somehow to be side-tracked then that was unfortunate but perhaps necessary. He put in a great deal of time and thought to the question of how the MD might be removed from the situation with dignity and without undue financial detriment, but then matters came to a head when the MD suddenly announced that he intended to acquire additional shares to give himself a majority holding, which he would use to drive through a number of reforms to the company, after which (he said) he would relinquish some of those shares and allow the ex-FD to take over the reins and step more or less into the MD role. Unfortunately, by now relations had deteriorated to the point where none of the other directors, S. included, was inclined to trust him, and this proposal was seen as merely a ruse to gain control of the company and undo everything that had been changed over the previous two years.

At this point the institution did something very sudden and unexpected. The investment controller appointed an outside consultant to look at the situation and report on the options. This move was not discussed beforehand with S. – indeed, there did not actually seem to be any plan to inform him about it. S. found out almost by accident when the controller slipped the information in during a discussion they were having (at S.'s request) about the current state of affairs, and was extremely unhappy at the way what had always seemed to be a strong and open relationship between the institution and himself was apparently being sidelined. The consultant came in, and soon sussed out the dynamics of the situation, but also recognized the potential for the company under the right management. As a result he recommended that *he* be appointed chief executive to lead it to a flotation, and by the way, he would want equity, options, and so on. It was difficult to avoid the impression that he suddenly saw an opportunity he liked.

Neither the ex-FD nor S. was particularly thrilled with this turn of events. The former felt that he held the key to the company's future success and that he didn't really need another outsider muscling in on the process. S. felt that the institutional investor had seriously undermined his own position as its nominee by not communicating with him about the consultant's appointment and remit; he further felt that the institution was in danger of actually undermining the board's integrity by its totally unilateral action. He also saw a danger that the board as presently constituted might become dysfunctional. He reported all this to the investment controller, and at the same time the ex-FD – with S.'s full knowledge and approval – put forward his own plan for the company's future. It was now probably apparent to the institution that there was no need (nor any desire) for an external presence to drive the situation forward, and in fact the consultant now faded somewhat from the scene, but the institution would say only that at this stage they would consider the ex-FD's plan and discuss it further with him and S. in due course.

It was, however, clear that relations between the MD and the rest of the board were breaking down completely, and that the rest of the board wanted him out. S. also took soundings among other senior managers, immediately below board level, and got the same feedback, namely that things would only really improve if the MD went. He took legal advice regarding the possibility of terminating the MD's employment – he had a contract with the company but there was in the articles of association a provision for terminating a director's appointment in certain circumstances. Accordingly, at the next board meeting S. over-rode the formal agenda and made a brief statement setting out his unhappiness with the state of affairs and saying that in his view the root of the problem lay with the MD. S. requested him to consider his position, and adjourned the meeting until the following morning. The MD then had one-to-one discussions with each director, including of course S. S. told him that he felt he should resign as MD but that he believed there was a role for him in the company's future, albeit probably not at director level.

That evening, the ex-FD and S. took further legal advice which confirmed to them that it was possible to terminate both the MD's employment and his directorship.

When the Board re-convened the following morning the MD presented a paper which, far from suggesting a fresh way forward, simply reiterated his own position and claimed that he was the victim of some sort of conspiracy. S. stated that the rest of the board no longer had any confidence in him, and invited him to resign. He refused. S. repeated the question twice, he refused twice, so a motion was put to the board for the termination of his appointment, which was carried with him in a minority of one.

The institution had been kept informed of all progress in the matter but had not offered any comment or any kind of steer – however, when S. reported the board's proceedings the investment controller said 'I don't think you should have done that!' Phrases about shutting stable doors after bolting horses sprang to S.'s mind. But the deed had been done: the staff were told, and in nearly every case the reaction was favourable (loud cheers went up in some places). However, over the ensuing few days the institution hesitated to give the move their backing – despite their earlier position of support for the ex-FD and S., S. was never given a wholly satisfactory explanation for this: somehow, phrases about 'undermining credibility by withdrawing support from someone whom we had backed at the time of the buy-out' rang a little hollow in the context of previous expressions of support for S. himself and the ex-FD.

Both the ex-FD and S. now felt that, notwithstanding what they had done, and in spite of the institution's previous statements in their favour, until they had unequivocal backing from the institution their position was potentially precarious because they couldn't be sure of commanding the support of a majority of shareholders. Consequently, although they did a lot of work on revised plans and budgets, they did not feel able to get all the staff together and give them a thorough formal briefing. But they did go round all the company's offices and speak to everybody on an informal basis, making clear why they had done what they had done and, in broad terms, how they saw the future. By and large their position seemed to be understood, even though they themselves were not wholly comfortable with it. However, some major moves were made in the direction of reshaping the company's structure and operating philosophy, and great efforts were directed towards gaining the support of its major financial backers. All of a sudden, the relationship with the joint venture partner also became smoother.

The ousted MD meanwhile requisitioned (as was his right) an extraordinary general meeting, which made it absolutely essential from the point of view of those now in charge that the 'new régime' could command majority support among the shareholders. Discussions were held with as many as possible, but one, a senior manager whose support until then had been rock-solid, was away on holiday and failed to return his voting paper. At first nobody was unduly concerned about this. S. had originally recruited the particular individual into the company, and had maintained a fairly close relationship with him, and indeed about five months previously he had urged S. (in a private discussion held at his request) to get rid of the MD and assume the role himself. As the days progressed, however, and the EGM date approached, an element of anxiety developed about the small percentage of the equity this manager owned which might make the difference between success and failure. At this stage the institution now, belatedly, came on board, saying that if the 'new' board could command a majority of the shareholders they would give it their backing, but it turned out to be too late. Somehow, the ousted MD managed to get the votes of the absentee manager on his side, which was sufficient to give him majority control, and two days before the EGM it was clearly all over.

The EGM itself was quite a bizarre affair: the ex-FD resigned the day before, rather than be voted out, and stayed away from the meeting. S. felt that he himself should be there (actually he was entitled to go anyway, as he held shares) but rather than give anyone the satisfaction of sacking him he resigned half-an-hour prior to the meeting, and attended in his capacity as a shareholder only. The institution's investment controller was there, and abstained on the motion to reinstate the former MD who, once reinstated, completely snubbed the controller – the institution was now seen as a dissident shareholder! To make matters even more strange, the manager who had 'swapped sides' actually left the company only a matter of weeks after all this happened, so it seemed anybody's guess what his motivation had been for the action he took – it certainly didn't appear to have been a promise of promotion.

So for S. it was rather a sudden end to a promising directorship, one which had involved just about all the roles and all the competencies discussed in Part I. It was all the more frustrating for having become so engrossing, for latterly it had taken up more or less all of S.'s time, and from being 'semi-executive' had become almost completely 'executive'. During it, he had achieved a lot for the company and its stakeholders, and the further prospects seemed exciting. In many respects, the company was knocking at the door of maturity: its systems were sound and robust, its structure was working well and beginning to develop new strengths, and many of its people were very nearly ready for greatly increased levels of responsibility. Much of S.'s input was directed towards helping all that to happen, and for a time all the conditions for it to happen were in place.

But he ended up out on his ear, so ultimately the judgement must surely be that he was unsuccessful. Maybe he had become too committed – maybe he should have taken a back seat, like his predecessor. But what value would that have added? That predecessor had just presided as chairman over a horrendous year's loss, so it's difficult to see how he had added any value. And once he was convinced that the MD was not the right person to take the company forward into full maturity, there is a strong argument to the effect that S. would not have been adding value by accepting his continued tenure. There could well be the accusation of disloyalty against S., of course, in the sense that he and the MD had developed a good relationship and S. subsequently not just undermined it but drove a coach-and-four through it: the response to that would have to be that S.'s responsibility was in the context of the company as a whole and he came to see the continued presence of the MD as detrimental to the company's future.

One possibility worth reflecting on is that S. may not have played the role of leader sufficiently strongly, and thereby may have allowed the initiative to pass for a time to the FD; this in fact was fatal to S.'s own position – firstly in terms of the perception of him held by the institution, and secondly in the sense that the agenda he might have pursued in possibly restructuring the company would have been different, less overtly confrontational, and therefore perhaps less likely to risk alienating people upon whom one would later seek to rely. S. readily admitted on subsequent reflection that everything began to happen sooner, and more quickly, than he had originally thought was appropriate: his own timescale had envisaged the MD going some four or five months later than what actually happened. But equally, it could be convincingly argued that the longer he was allowed to hang on, the more likely it would be that he would somehow thwart the plans for a restructuring, in which case the FD was right to precipitate things. Was there, though, a perception by the institution that S. had lost the initiative? Did he fall down on the networking? Was that why they engaged the consultant behind his back?

On the other hand, there may be an argument which says that in fact S. should have been more passive at that stage. Perhaps he over-reacted to the institution's apparent failure to communicate with him regarding the consultancy exercise, and should just have gone along with that. But S.'s point was that there was no way he could see how the consultant was going to input value that was not going to be provided in any case from elsewhere, so he saw no necessity or justification for that person's involvement, and certainly did not believe it was going to be in the interests of the shareholders as a whole for his exercise to proceed.

It is difficult to avoid the conclusion that in this instance the investing institution actually contributed in a major way to the fiasco: they clearly had some reservations about the MD at the time of S.'s appointment, and they certainly indicated on a fairly regular and consistent basis to

S. that they backed the various lines he was taking. He in turn took care to keep them informed as closely as practicable, and could probably have been forgiven for thinking that, as their nominee, he was entitled at least to be privy to their thinking as the situation developed. Yet despite the apparent support he had from the local director, the particular investment controller appeared to have no actual plan to inform him beforehand of their appointment of the consultant, and at the very end when their support was not forthcoming nobody was more surprised than S., especially considering the lack of any coherent and rational explanation. By that time of course the process leading to the termination of the MD's contract had been set in motion and it wasn't practicable to put a halt to it – indeed, significantly, the investment controller never actually suggested that S. should put a halt to it, and only demurred once it had been actioned. In the end, it was the vote of one senior member of staff (whom S. had originally encouraged to take up shares!) that swung it, so if there is any lesson to be drawn it must surely be that, however well things may seem to be going, and however much the course of a directorship may seem to be developing along sound and supportable lines, with roles and competencies in place and compatible, you should never take anything for granted, even the support of those you imagine to be the closest to you.

Summary of key points

Stage of company's evolution:	Maturity
Role/s played by non-exec:	Leader
	Mentor
	Confidant
	Thinker
	Doer
	Evaluator
	Networker
	Terminator
	Mole
Competencies required:	**Thinking** - all
	Getting results - all
	Influencing - all
	Self-managing - all

10

Specialist Clothing Manufacturer

This company made 'serious' outdoor clothing for walkers, climbers and similar types: it had been set up as a buy-out from the business empire of a fairly prominent public figure in a particular part of the country, and the buy-out funding included outside equity investment from two institutions and a major retail customer. F. was the second non-executive director since the company's establishment.

From small beginnings, the company had become extremely successful, thanks largely to its MD, the leader of the original buy-out, an energetic and highly-regarded salesman who was well-known in the market place served by the company. He was (as can so often happen) perhaps its greatest strength and its greatest weakness, for there was no-one of real stature below him in the company and things did revolve around him to an extent that was not totally healthy. As long as he was on song, everything was fine, but there is no telling what would have happened if he had fallen victim to the 'big red bus' or if his health had given way. Fortunately, nothing untoward did befall him, but it is worth noting that F. did from time to time feel uneasy at the extent to which everything depended on one person, creating an element of ongoing immaturity in what was in other respects a maturing company. Senior management (what little there was of it) consisted of individuals who were part of the 'serious outdoor' scene, which probably led to the company exhibiting and retaining the enthusiasm of youth, but at the same time the legacy of its previous existence as part of a large empire helped it to be less childish or adolescent than it might have been.

Although the company's products were very much aimed at enthusiasts, it benefited greatly for a number of years from the boom in sales of 'fleece' jackets to the general leisure market, and for a time seemed content to ride relatively passively on that bandwagon. When F. joined the board the company had just had its best-ever year, but things in the fleece market were showing signs of a slight slowdown and the company didn't have much else of general interest to punt towards leisure users (as distinct from the more specialist users) – indeed, it was in some danger of exhibiting something of a small company mentality in the sense that it was rather narrowly focused and had little vision of what it could become, while seeming to ignore the possibility that the good times might be coming to an end. In the meantime, however, it had amassed quite a substantial 'cash mountain' as a result of continuing profitability and a reluctance to spend any money on business development.

One of the characteristics of the business the company was in was its seasonality. The main camping and outdoor leisure trade shows are in the spring, when the manufacturers display their ranges for the next season. On the basis of what they see at the shows and in the catalogue produced around the same time, the buyers place their forward orders, for delivery mainly from September until November/December. So the manufacturers' peak period of activity tends to be from around Easter through till late autumn, but cash flow is likely to be negative until the retailers get their deliveries in September onward. Then, if particular lines sell well, customers may re-order for delivery in December/January, after which demand quietens down again until the spring trade shows. Clearly, therefore, much depends on a manufacturer's range being well-received, and you don't necessarily know how well your range is going to be received at the time when you are placing your orders with material suppliers (many of whom are overseas) and incurring your major debts – strong nerves are sometimes called for, as well as a high degree of confidence in your marketing abilities.

What would also be valuable would be a degree of counter-cyclicality (for example, by selling to the southern hemisphere where the seasons are the reverse of our own) or an independence from strict seasonality (for example, by producing lightweight garments that may be used during the summer months). Unfortunately, although the company had some success for a while with customers in Chile through a member of the managing director's family, most of the potentially biggest southern hemisphere markets were a bit impractical for it because of the costs of shipping, a situation exacerbated in the case of Australia and New Zealand by their proximity to countries in the Far East which were beginning to manufacture their own outdoor leisure garments at prices which seriously undercut anything a UK exporter could achieve. So F. started to press the case for lightweight waterproofs; at first, there wasn't much enthusiasm for the idea, but eventually the company designed and produced a range, and they sold very well – however, by now they were behind their competitors in the field, so their success was at first less than it might possibly have been, and sales took some time to build.

The cliché of a good big company always beating a good little one does, for the most part, hold true. Successful though it was, this company simply wasn't big enough in any of its areas of activity to be a world-beater – in fact, to be brutally honest it wasn't big enough to be anything other than a 'me-too' operation. It did not invest sufficiently in design (in fact, when F. joined the board it had no specialist dedicated designer in-house) to be known as an innovator, and although it was towards the 'technical' end of the outdoor clothing spectrum it nevertheless depended to a significant extent on sales to mainstream high street outlets and so could not afford to become too specialist. F. concluded, therefore, that it needed to be viewed as a less-than-long-term investment by the institutions, one which should perhaps be fattened up relatively quickly and sold. As it happened, this might not be totally incompatible with the priorities of the managing director, who by then was in his late fifties and likely to be looking for an exit within a period of five years or so.

Meanwhile, F. gave the MD what support he could: there were just the two of them on the board, so the MD was probably quite lonely at times, especially when the going was tough! F.'s main role was concerned with monitoring and advising on board processes and providing a 'sounding-board' for the MD, as well as doing some devil's advocacy when it came to reviewing and challenging some of the more conservative attitudes towards products and markets.

However, all of a sudden things were thrown into some ferment. F. happened to find out, from a quite separate and independent source, that Scottish Enterprise were reviewing their investment portfolio with a view to exiting from some companies and perhaps recycling the money into new investments. There also appeared to be a slight undercurrent in the form of a political feeling (this was the late 1980s to early 1990s) that perhaps equity investment wasn't what Scottish Enterprise should be about, though nobody ever admitted as much openly. After some enquiries it turned out that Scottish Enterprise had indeed been instructed by their masters at the Scottish Office to sell a proportion of their equity holdings, and that they had commissioned a firm of merchant bankers to carry out the sale. F. managed to obtain a copy of a list of the 'target' companies earmarked for disposal, and this particular company appeared on the list. Nobody, however, from the bankers, the Scottish Office, or indeed, Scottish Enterprise, had thought fit to inform the company of this.

This was obviously extremely rude, high-handed and arrogant. The notion – or at any rate, the perceived notion – that it didn't really matter to anyone in the company what a major shareholder did with their stake was quite unacceptable, and the MD and F. were furious. It also, however, had profound implications for the ongoing management of the business, for the possibility that a significant percentage of the equity might be about to change hands made it difficult to progress with the formulation of a strategic plan, since clearly the shareholders needed to be aware of the strategy and approve of it in principle. Moreover – and this was what really irritated F. and the MD, because it showed a total lack of professionalism on the part of the bankers – the company's articles of association provided for full pre-emption rights in the event of any shareholder wishing to divest of their shares, but this hadn't apparently been spotted by those charged with the task of selling, so not only were the directors not informed but neither were any of the other shareholders.

As it happened, F. knew someone in the Scottish Office quite well, so he agreed with the MD that he would use the contact to see if he could (a) get to the bottom of things, and (b) prevent anything precipitate from being done. Accordingly, F. spoke to his acquaintance and found out how to access the relevant corridor of power; eventually he had a meeting with the Scottish Office official ultimately responsible for Scottish Enterprise at which he made clear not only the company's annoyance at what had happened but also what they thought of the merchant bankers and their conduct. He tried to explain the impact on the company's progress (and possibly also its performance) as a result of the uncertainty which had been created, and to highlight the commercial implications as well as the behavioural ones. There was little in the way of formal response, and no apology, but they did subsequently hear that the whole exercise had been quietly but unceremoniously dropped.

Once this episode was over, the directors were able once again to give proper thought and attention to the company's strategy, and in particular to focus on how to work towards the MD's eventual exit; this was likely to be in a little over six years from then, so they felt that they should develop a plan aimed at maximizing value over such a period in order that the company might be as marketable as possible. It was recognized that although the company possessed quite a strong brand, it was in its present form too small (the turnover at the time was around £2.5 million) to be a really attractive purchase, and consequently some thought should be given in the direction of possible mergers or acquisitions in order to build it up – it was also recognized that such a course might possibly help to strengthen the company's management in that anything that was acquired might have something worthwhile in the way of a management resource. F. produced a paper setting out a suggested approach, together with criteria for acquisitions and a timescale which would see any such exercise completed and 'bedded down' in good time before the MD would wish to exit, and this was duly adopted as board policy (and duly notified to the investing institutions).

One or two possible opportunities cropped up, but nothing that was going to get anywhere near the flashpoint of heather, still less set it alight. Then, quite suddenly, news came to the directors about a company which had a factory less than five miles away, and whose range of products could be seen as complementary to theirs, which was in serious trouble – so serious that investigating accountants had been called in. It happened that one of the people looking at whether a rescue was on the cards was an accountant friend of F.'s, so F. was able to find out a little about the business, and it seemed there might be something worth considering, although a rescue as such did not look to be a realistic proposition. In the event, the company went into receivership, and F. and his colleagues did some hurried calculations and decided to approach the receiver with an offer.

It seemed to them that the company had a lot of what they were looking for. It had two good brand names, it had two product ranges of which one was closely related to the leisure-oriented end of their own range and the other was aimed at the countrywear market, it had management (though there had to be a question mark against their quality), and it had a modern factory which was at the time under-utilized and could therefore offer some useful additional capacity. There was obviously some doubt about its own viability, given the fate it had suffered, but on the face of it there did seem to be not only some kind of 'fit' with the acquiring business but also some added value.

The receiver was (as is so often true) looking for a quick sale, and time for diligence was strictly limited, especially as another possible bidder appeared in the form of a Scottish conglomerate with textile interests. They, however, pulled back and left the field open, and a deal was duly done. Most of the purchase price was met in cash, thanks to the 'mountain' mentioned previously, and apart from the odd hiccup, such as when it turned out that the receiver didn't actually have good title to one of the trade marks, the acquisition went through reasonably smoothly.

However, the new owners found that to a greater extent than had been apparent all was not well with the new business. Most of the senior management went, as part of the deal, and were not particularly sadly missed, but those who remained proved to be not much of an asset. The order book was weaker than everyone had been given to understand, as a result of poor marketing over a significant period, despite the apparent strength of the brands, and appeared to depend to an unhealthy extent on a number of franchise outlets in various parts of the country. In the United States, where F. and his colleagues had been led to believe that there was significant demand, capitalizing on the combination of 'Scottishness' and traditional outdoor wear, the agent was quite clearly not up to the mark. Finally, the workforce was less docile than the original company's, which might not have been a problem in itself but soon became one when they discovered that there was a fairly large wage differential in favour of the original company's employees. On the positive side, of course, the original company had acquired substantial additional manufacturing capacity at a time when strong demand for its own products had necessitated the use of costly sub-contract manu-facturing – though the scope for flexibility was undermined to an extent by the workforce problems referred to above.

Problems such as those just outlined are, if not inevitable, then certainly extremely likely in a 'distress sale' situation, and of course if you don't think you can cope then you shouldn't entertain the possibility of an acquisition in such circumstances. F. and his colleagues of course did not go into the process with their eyes shut, but clearly they had not realized beforehand quite how bad things were. Had they had more time to do the diligence, they might well have realized – but the reality is that you very often *do not have* a lot of time, particularly when a small business is being disposed of by a receiver, whose concern is only for the proceeds he can generate and how quickly he can generate them. The process also illustrated one of the limitations of the non-exec role: if the management of a company want badly enough to do something, it is unlikely that you can do a lot to stop them unless you can demonstrate convincingly that it will result in significant harm! In this case, the benefits appeared to outweigh the drawbacks, and time eventually showed this to be the case, but along the way there is no doubt that considerable strain was put on a very small management team, and F. later reckoned that if the same kind of situation were to arise again he would have reservations about proceeding in the same way.

The results of the acquisition were mixed. The two 'new' brands both under-performed significantly, due probably to inadequate marketing which was itself due to inadequate resources. The disappearance of the cash mountain meant that bank finance had to be utilized over the fol-lowing couple of years to an unprecedented extent, and this led to an unwillingness to invest in anything which would use up working capital. Harmonization between the product ranges took a while to achieve, so that for a number of years there was an element of duplication, particularly among fleeces and waterproofs, and a lack of brand clarity. On the other hand, once the anomalies in terms of employment had been ironed out, there was a huge gain in production flexibility and efficiency, the enlarged business was able to manufacture much more of its needs in-house, and profitability rose along with sales turnover.

Partly as a result of the increased workload arising from the acquisition and from the recognition that it was now a much bigger company, F. became instrumental in persuading the MD to strengthen the board by appointing a sales director and a financial director – both from within the company – and this helped to ease some of the burden on the MD as well as increasing the effectiveness of governance. However, none of this did much to solve the underlying problems of still being a relatively small player in a market in which some very big mergers were beginning to take place; and of course the MD's eventual aim was still to exit (as was that of the outside shareholders).

A potential purchaser suddenly appeared some three or four years after the acquisition just described. Immediately the MD was put under intense pressure – the approach was friendly, but the indicative offer was not particularly generous and the bidder's advisers were a firm of accountants whose corporate style is well known as being that of continuous hustling. They pushed for a quick deal, setting quite unrealistic time schedules and pestering the MD daily by phone, whilst he tried to conduct things in a more measured and rational manner. The institutional shareholders were quite keen for a quick deal, the other outside shareholder slightly less so in view of the apparent lack of generosity.

F. now found himself treading the fine line between representing the institutions and trying to safeguard the interests of the MD, his family, and the other shareholders, not to mention the rest of the senior management team, particularly the recently-appointed sales director. There was no doubt in F.'s mind that, in an owner-managed company, ethics demanded that the first priority must be to satisfy the reasonable needs and objectives of the owner–manager/s. As pointed out earlier, however, this is fine as long as these do not conflict in any way with what the institutions want! The problem can arise if and when one party's needs and objectives change – if the target timescale for an exit changes, for example, or if indeed the wish for an exit itself is somehow compromised. Years ago, 3i in particular made a great play about their desire to see owner–managers' wishes fulfilled, and publicly tended to subordinate their own agenda to this. More recently, however, and especially since they became a PLC, 3i's agenda has changed, in order to reflect the need to maximize short-term shareholder value, and there was no doubt in F.'s mind that the same kind of shift in attitude was evident in the briefings he got from the investment controller regarding the possible disposal of this company. F. himself was far from convinced that the deal on offer represented the best value for the MD, but as the institutions' nominee he was expected to toe a party line which said 'sell'.

In point of fact, although the deal on offer was not brilliant, it came at a time when the company's fortunes were slipping somewhat. For the previous two years, the largest single customer had been a Japanese trading company whose purchases had grown to the extent that it accounted for almost 20 per cent of the company's sales. That particular year, the economic problems in Japan began to catch up on it, and the bulk order was reduced by some 60 per cent in value from the previous year's. At the same time, one of the other major Far East customers, in South Korea, effectively ran out of money and couldn't pay for their goods other than by a 'contra' arrangement involving purchases of some items manufactured by them. The Hong Kong customer almost went bust and the Singapore customer also ran into difficulties. Indeed, of their entire Far Eastern customer base (collectively by far the largest group of customers they had) only that in Taiwan remained buoyant. In fact, the company suffered a kind of 'triple whammy', for as well as the collapse of their Far East market they also found their sales to many European countries hit by the strength of sterling, and an abnormally dry and mild winter not only devastated their season but also of course had a knock-on effect in that the new season's prospects didn't look too promising as many shops still had previous season merchandise to sell and weren't too interested in taking on large volumes for the new season.

The upshot of all this was that the bidder actually reduced his offer price to a level some way below what any of the shareholders was prepared to accept, and the board broke off negotiations (with the full though regretful support of the institutional shareholders). There was an abortive attempt at a buy-in, almost two years later, which fell apart when the backers decided that the gearing would be unacceptably high. The company soldiered on; the MD was by now past the age at which he wanted to retire, so he reduced his role to become part-time chairman and a new MD was recruited. He had some strong ideas about refocusing the company's efforts, but it was clearly going to take some considerable time to rebuild its fortunes.

Eventually a possible way forward appeared, in the shape of a merger with another company in a similar field whose product range in fact complemented theirs. It too was in some difficulty, so the potential economies offered by putting the two together were quite attractive, as well as, of course, the obvious commercial synergy. The financing of the merger wasn't especially easy because none of the institutional share-holders wanted to invest further (though at the same time they had no wish to pull out and wreck everything), but the business plan was sufficiently attractive and robust for suitable medium-term financing to be found. As part of the reorganization, F. came off the board after some nine years as a non-exec.

This company, and F.'s involvement in it as a non-executive director, illustrated from the start many of the peculiarities of the SME, both positive and negative. It was in fact relatively mature, but it lacked any depth of management. It partly compensated for this by being extremely good at what it did, producing a range of products of high quality which were targeted at a number of retail outlets with which excep-tionally good relations were maintained. The prevailing ethos, however, was deeply conservative, and the company actually ran the risk of slipping into premature old age, although thankfully its management style never in fact ossified to quite that extent. But it fell into the trap early on of not investing sufficiently in its own future in terms of development of products and systems, and once it did begin to invest, and grow, there was a danger of it not actually capitalizing on its own success. It is difficult to avoid the conclusion that a more dynamic management might have made more out of the acquisition that took place, and not been quite so content to reason afterwards that it had been little more than 'a worthwhile expansion of production facilities' – though, of course, that was in fact a very real benefit in terms of lessening reliance on outside sub-contractors.

However, it is necessary to take cognizance of what was referred to earlier as 'the psychology' of an SME, and in particular of the family-owned business. An investing institution of course has its own agenda related to a pre-determined formula for growth in value and rate of return, which is fine, but such an agenda is not necessarily in complete harmony with that of the owner–managers. As a non-exec it is important to realize where the congruences and differences are and to have a fairly firm view about them which you can defend if necessary *either* to the owner–managers *or* to the institutions. If your view isn't well-formed you may well not make your optimum contribution to the company because you will tend to be fighting fires all the time without a strategic overview. Where there is – as here – a single owner–manager, the agenda can be clearer than if there are several who may differ among themselves about absolute objectives, but because that agenda will essentially be of a personal nature it may be more difficult to reconcile with any outside shareholders' priorities.

Where the priorities of more than one outside shareholder conflict, as happened here when Scottish Enterprise tried to offload, the non-exec must stand up and be counted and must have regard to the interest of probity and commercial integrity even if that means speaking out against an institution by whom he has been, or has hopes of being, sponsored.

Thus, notwithstanding the somewhat low-key eventual outcome, the value that F. added to this particular company lay in the way he took a leading role in seeking to reconcile the wishes of external and internal shareholders, in being a networker and using contacts to fight battles when necessary, and in being an evaluator and helping to bring about a more 'managerial' style and ethos, trying to nudge the company towards maturity while avoiding the danger of premature old age. He was also, especially in the early years, a confidant to a somewhat lonely MD. All of these did help in some way to enhance any ultimate value in the business, though external circumstances meant that it would be some considerable time before that climbed again to the kind of level that had at one time seemed possible. However, the company did retain a worthwhile reputation and an element of desirability which certainly made it a potentially viable merger partner at a time when the market was very depressed, and helped to make the post-merger business plan credible. F. was on the board for nine years, which is probably too long for a non-exec, and it is ironic to reflect that if he had left sooner he might have been associated only with the success of its middle years, before its problems began.

Summary of key points

Stage of company's evolution:	Adolescence, approaching Maturity, slight danger of premature Old Age
Role/s played by non-exec:	Confidant
	Thinker
	Doer
	Evaluator
	Networker

Summary of key points   (*continued*)

Competencies required: **Thinking**   - all

Getting results - Initiative
- Results focus
- Determination
- Critical information seeking
- Concern for standards

Influencing   - Concern for impact
- Persuasiveness
- Organizational awareness
- Strategic influencing
- Relationship building

Self-managing   - Independence
- Self-development
- Positive self-image
- Flexibility
- Organizational commitment

11
Engineering Design Consultancy

This was a new start, invested in by a local office of a venture capital organization who put B. forward as nominee director. The moving force behind it was an engineer with specialist experience in water treatment, and his original idea was to design and, where practicable, to manufacture control systems and equipment for the water and sewage industry. This was in fact very timely: the water supply and sewage treatment sectors had fairly recently been privatized, and some of the companies that had been created – such as Anglian, Severn-Trent, and so on – were highly profitable and at the same time coming under pressure to spend lots of money on new plant. There was clearly, then, a major opportunity on offer to someone with the means to exploit it.

The founder of the company took in with him another shareholder–director, a colleague from their previous employer, but this was by no means a partnership of equals. The MD was not the easiest of people to get on with, and he had little patience with anyone he saw as being inferior or less dynamic. He treated his fellow director, in fact, as something of a half-wit, and sometimes it was a matter for some wonder why he'd ever teamed up with him in the first place. They did, however, seem to make a surprisingly effective team and there was clearly a favourable perception of them in the industry. At first, they operated out of a small serviced office, but after a few months the company moved into new premises consisting of a small office suite with a factory behind it, and so were able to start manufacturing.

B.'s role was seen primarily as that of advising on 'the right way' to do things – such items as internal systems, structures, quality assurance procedures, and so on, as is frequently the case with a non-exec role in a brand-new company – but he also got very involved in the relationship between the MD and the venture capitalists. As it happened, the MD and the particular investment controller got on reasonably well, and after a year or so there was a second round of financing in which the particular institution participated, expressing a degree of confidence in the company and its management team. However, some time after this the controller moved away to work in a different office of the venture capital company in a different part of the country, and the relationship with his successor was considerably less easy. Quite why this should be the case was by no means clear: probably the MD's personality was a factor, but it did seem to B. that the new investment controller's overall attitude was not very supportive, and that neither this new controller nor anyone else in the local office seemed any longer to understand what the business was all about (the local director of the venture capital company having also changed since the original investment). B. found himself in effect in a new environment, having to work extremely hard to keep relations between the investors and the company on an even keel, and to maintain a balance between being perceived by the former as 'going native' and being perceived by the latter as a spy for the venture capital organization!

The company traded reasonably well in its early days, although profits proved depressingly difficult to sustain. Project work is notoriously unreliable at yielding consistent profits, largely because when the costing and estimating are done beforehand the extent of provision that should be made for contingencies is, to be blunt, a matter of guesswork – and especially so if you are going to be reliant almost totally on third parties for the actual execution of the project. So the company tended to make money on manufacturing control panels but not to make much on the design and project management side.

However, good relations were established with most of the major water companies, so there was a steady flow of business and the company expanded – this too put pressure on margins, although it must be said that the expansion was controlled and did not happen at a ridiculous rate. The second shareholder–director, as might perhaps have been foreseen, very quickly got left behind as the business developed, and after a bit of pressure volunteered to sell his shares to the MD and to leave the company. This did not go down well with the institution, however, who quite understandably did not wish to see only one shareholder–director. Fortunately, another potential participant came into view at the time: an engineer with a pump manufacturing company, who was willing to join the company and purchase the previous director's shares. He lived in another part of the country, nearer to where most of the company's major customers were located, so it was decided to open a second office there and for him to become a director of the company based at that office. That, too, consumed part of what might otherwise have been profit, but the MD and the non-exec both regarded it as a potentially worthwhile investment, given the geographical factor just mentioned, and the institution concurred with such a view.

For a while things were very promising and despite the still-inconsistent pattern of profitability, and the slightly uneasy relationship with the investment controller, everybody was quite bullish about prospects. An export order was won to manufacture a series of control panels for the water industry in Pakistan, and on the design side some prestigious business came the company's way related to major new treatment works in the south of England. The company took a stand at the industry exhibition at the National Exhibition Centre; B. spent a day there to see for himself how the company related to others in the water industry, and was impressed at the extent to which they were highly regarded by many key individuals in the various supply companies who had the authority to award business.

A few months later, however, things suddenly became fraught. There was slippage in the timetable on a project, resulting as far as B. could see from a lack of attention to detail in the way the branch office had planned things, and extra resources had to be put into resolving the situation. This meant, in turn, that a second project became under-resourced and subject to delays, and all of a sudden there was a danger of a domino type of situation. More seriously, because the projects were generating cash on a stage-payment basis, delays were costly and started to affect the company's cash flow. At the same time, to make matters worse, the bankers quite suddenly and unexpectedly became less supportive. They had on previous occasions allowed temporary increases to the overdraft to cover troughs in the cash flow; now, however, far from allowing increases they started threatening to cut the facility.

B. had quickly to take stock of the situation. On the one hand, if he thought the company could trade through its problems then he felt he ought to support its efforts; on the other hand, if there was a likelihood that it would fail he was under an obligation to do what he could to safeguard the interests of its stakeholders. B. felt that on the whole the actions of the bank did not seem to be justified in the circumstances – indeed, he and the other directors had a meeting with the bank manager and tried to find out from him why he had acted as he had, but failed to get a satisfactory answer.

Overall, B. concluded that the balance of merit for his support lay with the MD. Although, as pointed out previously, he wasn't the easiest of people to get on with, he was thoroughly competent and professional at his job, and with him at the helm B. believed that the company had a good future – although there would clearly need to be some reorganization at the branch office to ensure that projects were planned and handled better thereafter (a requirement which the MD thoroughly understood and accepted). B. reported and discussed this in some detail with the investment controller, whose response was non-committal, which seemed a little odd to B. After all, the local office had clearly been perfectly glad to cite this particular company as one of their notable investments – photograph on the office wall of the principals at the signing ceremony when the original deal was done, framed press cuttings, and so on – but somehow it now seemed they were no longer interested. B. thought this worrying because it was also clear to him that if the bank carried on in the way it was now acting the company's situation would quickly deteriorate irrespective of how well or otherwise the directors were handling matters, and that would obviously increase the pressure on him as the non-executive director.

Soon the bank started leaning heavily on the MD, demanding personal guarantees as the price for their continued support. He absolutely refused to go down this route, and B. supported him totally in this. B's rationale was, first, that he didn't believe that the bank's security position was being actually undermined; second, that the company's situation was redeemable, in the sense that it wasn't a case of its sales collapsing, rather a case of delayed cash intake which could be, and was now being, solved by action the company itself had taken; and thirdly, that it was the bank's precipitate action in turning unfriendly that had undermined the directors' confidence in its good faith – and if you can't rely on someone's good faith then you should *never, ever*, put yourself in a vulnerable position in relation to them.

Throughout all that was going on, B. made sure that he kept the investment controller well briefed and up-to-date with events, and of course he reported in detail the discussions that took place regarding guarantees. He then suggested that perhaps it would make sense for the controller to speak to the bank manager, on the one hand to try to find out where exactly the bank was coming from, and on the other hand to get across a message of the institution's continuing support for the company and its management, which might possibly provide some comfort for the bank. He got a vague and somewhat equivocal response, which he found unsettling and unsatisfactory. It appeared that the controller appeared unable to confide in him about what the investing institution really wanted to do about the situation, and he found this extremely difficult to accept – he was the institution's nominee on the company's board, after all – and felt that it put him in a very exposed position. Perhaps they believed that he had gone completely native, perhaps they saw him to an extent as a relic from a previous local administration and as such not 'one of them', perhaps they had just lost confidence in all the team. B. really had no way of knowing, and got no lead or steer whatsoever from the institution. So he followed his own judgement and gave the MD as much support as was practicable.

It wasn't enough. Cheques began to be bounced, suppliers were becoming increasingly nervous, and there seemed no way in which any meaningful reassurance could be given to them. The bank now demanded an expression of assurance from the institution as a condition for continuing the overdraft facility, the institution refused point-blank to give any such assurance, and the bank withdrew the facility. A receiver was appointed and there was a somewhat alcrimonious end to the relationship between B. and the investing institution's local office.

What went wrong? Did B. get too involved, should he have stood further back? Could he have done anything which might have led to a different outcome? It seems difficult in this case to identify anything specific which could have made a difference, because to all intents and purposes the company was not badly managed – it was brought down by one problem or group of problems which in fact *could* have been overcome if everyone had been prepared to lend their support. B. was fairly close to the MD and acted as his advocate as far as possible; perhaps he was perceived as having got *too* close to the MD, and, instead, he should have been more sensitive to the developing situation between the MD and the investing institution. In B.'s defence, he would certainly have claimed that he was in fact sensitive to it but for some reason was unable to get the investment controller 'on message'. He never was let into the secret of the controller's attitude, and this only reinforced his frustration. The corporate stance of the institution in question at that time was very much that they were 'hands-off' investors, in which case B. was surely justified in thinking that it would have been logical for the controller to come clean with him and explain their thinking.

The most obvious conclusion is that both the institution and the company's bank lost confidence in the MD and in his ability to weld the business together into something coherent. There is no doubt that it wasn't a particularly mature company, in spite of its good reputation among its customers, and perhaps the element of strain in the relationships with its financial backers contributed to the loss of confidence. However, if that was indeed the case then perhaps the sensible course of action would have been for the backers to tell that to the non-exec and discuss with him what might be done. In reality, however, neither the investment controller nor the bank manager was prepared to tell B., nor to respond to requests to discuss any aspect of the matter, so in the circumstances he had to follow his own judgement, and once he had done so he believed (with some justification) that he ought to see it through. He was trusted by the company and its officers, and while he was there he did in fact add value as confidant, thinker and evaluator. What seemed to happen was that a series of failures in communications involving third parties totally undermined everything he had done, and in the end the limitations of his role were exposed, for he was unable to influence events in a favourable direction.

It is of course just possible that, in the final analysis, B. turned out to be too hands-off and should have tried to become more involved in what was going on – perhaps, by making the project management side more effective. Possibly this might have built the confidence of the outside parties and allowed the company to grow out of its adolescence into the maturity of which it ought to have been capable. But this could most probably not have been achieved without the active co-operation of other parties involved – the bank manager and the investment controller – and there is no evidence to suggest that that co-operation would have been readily forthcoming. Unfortunately nobody is ever likely to know the answer, so the status of this case in terms of the fundamental thesis of this book is uncertain.

Summary of key points

Stage of company's evolution:	Childhood – Adolescence
Role/s played by non-exec:	Confidant
	Thinker
	Doer
	Evaluator
	Networker
	? Mole
Competencies required:	**Thinking** - all
	Getting results - Initiative
	- Thoroughness

	- Determination - Critical information seeking - Concern for standards
Influencing	- Concern for impact - Organizational awareness - Strategic influencing - Situational sensitivity
Self-managing	- Independence - Self-development - Positive self-image - Flexibility - Organizational commitment

12
Light Engineering Company

This was a management buy-out from an American company, financed jointly by 3i and the then Scottish Development Agency (later Scottish Enterprise). The company employed around 80 people and manufactured items for the electronics sector, its customers being principally in the field of telecommunications. The company itself actually had a fairly long history, having been a locally-grown business for a number of years prior to being taken over by the US corporation; after several years the American parent had decided that it no longer wished to manufacture in the UK and indicated its intention to close down. A couple of senior managers approached the institutions to enquire about the possibility of mounting a buy-out, and along the way a potential board of four people willing to invest their own money was put together and a business plan commissioned. A deal was agreed involving equity from these four and from the two outside institutions mentioned, plus a bank facility. The deal involved a 'ratchet' in that it gave the owner–managers initially 30 per cent of the ordinary equity but allowed them the opportunity to see this proportion raised to 70 per cent if certain profit targets were met in the early years of the new company's life. Part of the institutional funding was, as is usual in buy-outs, in the form of redeemable preference shares with a five-year target period for redemption.

When G. was first introduced to the about-to-be-inaugurated board, it was one or two days before the actual signing of the deal, and there was a fair amount of suspicion about him. The owner–managers thought he might be some kind of spy, or else a third party aiming to 'muscle in' on their new company, and it took a bit of time and effort to convince them that his intended role was in fact benign. However, he was accepted, and was nominated as chairman. This was a good thing in that he was in fact able in due course to demonstrate that there was a need for someone – preferably an outsider – to chair board meetings, because otherwise in the early days there would just have been endless arguments. The four executive directors were each competent, but together they constituted a most unlikely team, and none of them had any actual experience of being a director. There were certain tensions between the four as individuals, with one of them in particular being regarded (rightly, in G.'s view) as something of a lightweight – he was full of bluff and bluster, but in terms of relative contribution to the company's success he was in bottom position. However, his money was as good as anyone else's, and it was that which guaranteed him his seat on the board.

The other unusual feature of the board was that only two of the four owner–directors were actually based locally and, for that matter, employees of the company. The other two lived further south – one near Manchester, the other in Surrey – from where they ran sales operations as self-employed agents for the company and came to the company's premises for a few days each month around the time of the board meeting. G. often wondered, then and afterwards, whether this in fact helped to make things go smoothly, for if they had all been working together at close quarters all the time then they might have fallen out in a big way!

Because it was a relatively inexperienced board of directors (and this also applied to G.: this was only his third or fourth appointment to a non-executive directorship) there was an extent to which they were all 'feeling their way', and in the early days G. used to get together quite frequently with the financial director, who was one of the two 'home-based' directors, to agree on the next meeting's agenda and how the various items should be approached and dealt with. This led to a high degree of 'structuring' of the board meetings, probably more so than would normally be encountered in a company of comparable size, and in this instance it worked well. (Although it is by no means certain that it would necessarily always work, in *any* situation, it certainly did here.) It meant that each director knew quite clearly what he was going to have to answer for at the meeting, with the result that he was almost always well-prepared and the discussions which took place were generally informed rather than off-the-wall.

Being a buy-out from an American firm, the 'new' company had proper systems and procedures right from the start, and there was little need for G. to become involved in such areas apart from ensuring that these were reviewed as and when necessary. Rather, his focus was initially on setting standards for the board's operation and ensuring that these were developed and maintained – regular reporting formats, timetabling of issues, and so on. He did not get involved in operational matters unless this was felt to be appropriate as a kind of last resort, for example when on one occasion they had to declare a redundancy during a period of difficult trading and it was felt that the matter was sufficiently serious for *the chairman* to address the employees, and when on another occasion there was a problem with the union and G. was wheeled in to speak on behalf of the investors to underline management's position. He did, however, get involved with the company's strategy formulation, and in fact they developed what was for a small company a reasonably sophisticated planning structure.

The company was commercially extremely successful. Sales grew over a seven year period from less than £3 million to about £8 million, and apart from one difficult year (in which the whole industry suffered) they were very profitable – indeed, its rate of profitability was quite outstanding for a manufacturing company. Interestingly, in its very success it epitomized much of what 'popular capitalism' in the 1980s was all about. There were four hard-working managers, each able and willing to take something of a risk in financing their own company, with of course a view to a big pay-back somewhere down the line. There were the institutions backing them equally looking to a big pay-back. The overriding agenda was therefore fixed – build up the value as quickly as possible, then exit profitably – and everything else was more or less subordinated to it. Salaries were reasonable but not over-generous, and company car policy was conservative, so neither of these would undermine ongoing profitability. The boardroom was refurbished about a year or so after the buy-out, but not extravagantly, and the only mild concession to a 'lifestyle' was the annual sales conference the company held, which most years took place at an upmarket location in the south of England. At the same time, however, investment in R & D was minimal, as was investment in plant and equipment. So, up to a point, the longer term was sacrificed for the sake of the shorter. Meanwhile, the dividend stream for the institutions was very good, the preference shares were all redeemed ahead of schedule, and the 'ratchet' operated fully within about half the period originally envisaged in the company's articles of association. Thus from more or less every point of view it was very successful within this fairly narrow agenda of growth over a finite period followed by a sale – in other words, there was no commitment to a longer term. It could be argued that this sort of attitude is actually slightly worrying, for the sake of the aggregate added value nationally, and certainly G. had some personal misgivings on that score, but in the particular circumstances as a non-exec it was important for him to recognize what made them all tick, for after all it was their money, not his, which was at stake, and his job was to help them to maximize their return – as well, of course, as that of the investing institutions. When he got the chance, he made the case for a more liberal approach to employment issues, appealing to self-interest if nothing else on the basis that satisfied employees were more likely to deliver good performances and hence profits, but ultimately the non-exec has to accept that he can influence but not dictate.

As mentioned earlier, there was only really one difficult year during G.'s period with the company. The whole industry in fact suffered, but this particular company perhaps less than most because, as soon as the first signs of a slowdown occurred, the board took action, freezing wages and salaries (including those of the directors) and declaring a limited redundancy. Nor did they let customers and suppliers off the hook – suppliers were informed that they could no longer expect payment within any less than 60 days, whilst customers were pressed to settle their accounts as quickly as possible. Whether it was the result of being so 'up-front' about it all was never really known, but they got away with it and protected their cash flow to an amazing degree. In due course, the sector recovered, but the company made no attempt to change its cash policies, with the result that for most of the time after that they were in credit at the bank.

About four years after the buy-out they took over another company, buying the business from the receiver. Although its market was in a totally different sector, the basic business was, like that of the original company, metal-bending, so they had to learn a whole new set of market knowledge but at the same time were able to apply their production expertise to create an efficient operation and to make use of the additional manufacturing facilities. This synergy was used to underpin the decision-making process surrounding the takeover, and was a good example of a small company applying big company thinking, something which does not by any means always happen in such circumstances!

During G.'s chairmanship he also got involved in a couple of other interesting exercises. First, the company was approached by the Scottish Office and asked to take part in a project in which they were seeking to appoint some of their brightest 'rising stars' as non-execs to the boards of SMEs for a specific period of time in order to broaden their experience and try to avoid their becoming too insular and civil service-bound. This was a tremendous idea, one which one might wish would occur to more employers. In the event, the company took two such people in succession, each for a couple of years, one from the Industry Department and one from Agriculture and Fisheries. They both made a significant contribution: they were formidably bright, which meant that they were able to grasp relatively quickly the issues the board had to tackle and could make a worthwhile input. The fact that they came steeped in a totally different culture and method of working meant that they tended to question much of what was done and the assumptions on which various actions were based, and this of course put the rest of the directors on the spot and made them think that much harder about what they were doing and why they were doing it. The two civil servants both reckoned they also gained a lot from the experience.

The second project was a trade investment. Two men who worked for a metal stockist, from whom the company purchased much of its raw material, brought along a business proposition. The company was part of a national organization and had decided to close down its local branch, and these two guys decided to try to set up their own business to capitalize on the customer base that had been built up and was now about to be abandoned. After some deliberation, it was decided that they were worth backing and the company agreed to put money into their venture. They were pointed in the direction of good lawyers and accountants, and an arrangement was set up with them to purchase material from their company once it was set up. G. was nominated as chairman of the new company, acting as representative of the investor, in much the same way as he was investor nominee chairman of the original company. So once again he found himself helping to establish structures and procedures, as well as teaching new people how to be directors, only this time he also had to report to the main board on the performance of the investee company.

The new company broke even after a year, and in its second year had an opportunity to acquire another company which was part-competitor, part-complementary: G. drove the acquisition, which although it took longer than anticipated (owing principally to attitude problems on the part of the vendor) was finally successful. So now there they all were, a group, with a wholly-owned subsidiary *and* an associate company with its own subsidiary.

At about this time, one particular customer was going like a proverbial train. The market in which they were operating was entering what seemed like an unstoppable boom, and the company found itself being carried along on a wave of apparently exponential expansion. It had to increase its manufacturing capacity, which it did both organically and by making a further acquisition, this time of a jobbing-type engineering company nearby whose owner wanted to retire. The particular customer referred to above was soon accounting for well over 50 per cent of total sales. Great while it lasts, of course, but that sort of situation makes you somewhat vulnerable, and the directors did feel that sooner or later it must come to an end, and there was a measure of uncertainty as to how geared up they really were to find sales to compensate for any drop that might come. Moreover, it was now some seven years since the buy-out, and the oldest of the owner–directors had begun to think in terms of an exit. Given the track record they had now established, and the prospect of perhaps a couple more bumper years, it seemed increasingly that the time was right to look at the exit option. So, after a 'beauty parade', they selected a corporate finance firm to act on the company's behalf in seeking an acquirer.

G. was in fact quite genuinely surprised by how difficult this search seemed to be. At first, there was no shortage of companies apparently interested, but one by one they seemed to lose interest and in the end nobody made an offer. Then suddenly an offer came, more or less out of the blue, from a PLC considerably smaller than the would-be acquisition. Yes, they were really going places, yes, they would have no difficulty in putting together a deal, yes, they had access to serious funding. The chemistry between the owner–directors and the MD of the PLC's principal operating subsidiary was good, and before long discussions were at quite a serious level. However, they then found themselves exposed for the first time to the quite different, and to them quite alien, world of the PLC and its requirements in terms of disclosures, shareholder relations, and so on. What happened was that the PLC needed a rights issue in order to finance the proposed acquisition, and its main shareholders refused to underwrite that issue, for reasons which did not *in themselves* concern the directors of the potential acquisition but which, obviously, rather undermined any possible deal. So it was back to the drawing board.

Finally, some months afterwards, a possible deal presented itself which looked more robust. A man appeared on the scene with money, and gained the ear of an investment controller at a venture capital outfit. The plan was to acquire the company of which G. was chairman, acquire at the same time another company whose owner was also looking to exit, then merge the two companies and build a group by rapid acquisitions over a short period of time which was then to be floated, netting mega profits for management and backers. G. did not take to this person at all, and was far from sure that he would have backed him with his own money. The individual had worked in the United States for some time and the impression from his track record was that he seemed to have found himself in the right place at the right time when a company needed the sort of input he could provide, with the result that he had significant success to his credit and had in the process made a considerable amount of money personally. Now he said he wanted to settle back in his native land and get a multiplier on his money. G. was a little uneasy about it all – the man 'talked a good game' and that can very easily arouse suspicions because the more people like that talk the more difficult it usually becomes to get hold of the *substance* of what they are about. G. saw no real evidence that he actually knew how to manage a business: he was quite clearly going for the 'big picture', so whatever success he achieved would be likely to depend very much firstly on luck, and secondly on the quality of people he had round him. Moreover, it was also quite clear that what he was after was a quick profit, and it wasn't going to worry him at all how many toes he trod on in the process.

Did all this matter? He clearly won over the investment controller in a major way, and a potential deal was put together which appealed to G.'s fellow directors and to the institutions. G. was unable to point to anything tangible which was likely to be accepted as a risk of derailment, so he decided to keep his opinion to himself. If the owner–directors' financial aspirations were going to be met, as well as those of the investing institutions, then whether or not *the non-exec* liked the buyer, and whether or not he thought that buyer would deliver to *his* backers, was not particularly relevant. (Had G. been a potential nominee director for those backers, of course, the situation would have been different and it would have been legitimate, not to say important, for him to voice his opinion.)

In the process of completing the deal, various people were trampled on, including to an extent G. The metal stockist company in which the company held a stake and of which G. was chairman had a provision in its articles of association that the investor company had the right to appoint and dismiss its chairman – so, not surprisingly, it was decided that G. should be replaced by a nominee of the new régime. Perfectly right, of course, but at the same time the incoming MD decided that a director's fee which had just been awarded to G. by the metal stockist company in respect of the year just ended should instead be remitted to the investor company. There was no requirement for this in the articles, nor did there seem to be any justification apart from an apparent desire to prove his masculinity by showing just who was the boss. The other directors of the metal stockist company supported G., so in fact he was able to get a cheque paid and banked before the new régime was able to prevent it.

Interestingly, the newly-formed group didn't live up to all the hype and expectations its founders had raised. Sales and profitability were sluggish and below what had been projected, and some further financing was required; in addition the metal stockist company was sold to its management to raise cash. A number of unsuccessful attempts at acquisitions were made before one was finally successful: even then, however, performance lagged behind predictions. Eventually, after three years, an American company came along with an offer which the shareholders felt they couldn't refuse, even though the net gain was considerably less than the figures which had been waved in front of investors three years earlier. So, once again, there was no commitment to any long term: it will be interesting to see whether history repeats itself and the new American owner decides in the fullness of time that it no longer wishes to manufacture in the UK.

This particular directorship combined many of the sometimes contradictory characteristics that have been referred to at various points in this book. It began as a quite clearly hands-off appointment in an essentially mature company – almost aggressively hands-off, taking into account the initial attitudes of the members of the buy-out team! G. achieved what he did achieve by influence, not by direction, there being no question that the management team lacked any of the required day-to-day skills in running the company. Yet, at the same time, it was clearly recognized that he was in a position to contribute some things, both as a thinker and as a doer, which nobody else on the board could, and that overall the company was stronger with him than without him. When it came to the investment in the metal stockist, and to the subsequent building-up of that company and its own journey along the acquisition trail, everyone was perfectly happy for G. to be extremely hands-on and the value which he was able to add in that regard, as well as in being evaluator and mentor in that company, was universally recognized.

So it was in fact a successful and agreeable association. The manner of its ending was less agreeable, but that wasn't really the fault of anyone on the original board, unless of course their desire to do the deal with the particular buyer can be called a 'fault'. G. strongly believed that it was not in his place to question the credentials or the ability to deliver of the guy who came in, because whatever else he might or might not achieve he clearly was going to deliver to G.'s colleagues and investors. (However, G. did make the point that if the deal had not been proposed in cash but had involved for example an earn-out or an exchange of shares, then he would have been much less happy for the owner–directors and the investors, and would have expressed his unease.) The longer term interests of stakeholders, especially the employees, may be said to have been to an extent sacrificed, but it is probably legitimate to argue that they were sacrificed from Day 1 in terms of the thinking behind the original buy-out, and in a sense all that was happening was that the spirit of the times was guiding the way the deal was set up. The 'enterprise culture' tended to concentrate on short-term gains rather than long-term building, and it is not necessarily appropriate to knock an individual instance just for being part of and reflecting that culture.

Overall, G. was able to add significant value throughout his time with the company. He was, though, a horse for two different courses – and nowhere was this shown up in greater relief than when the sale came, for he spent a considerable amount of time with the metal stockist directors, explaining how it would all affect them and their company, and has since remained friendly with them even though unconnected, whereas he had absolutely no locus whatever in the discussions about the takeover of the parent company.

Summary of key points

Stage of company's evolution:	Maturity	
Role/s played by non-exec:	Leader	
	Mentor	
	Thinker	
	Doer	
	Evaluator	
	Networker	
Competencies required:	**Thinking**	- all
	Getting results	- Initiative
		- Results focus
		- Thoroughness
		- Determination
		- Critical information seeking
		- Concern for standards
		- Developing people

Influencing	- Concern for impact
	- Persuasiveness
	- Organizational awareness
	- Strategic influencing
	- Situational sensitivity
Self-managing	- Independence
	- Self-development
	- Positive self-image
	- Flexibility
	- Organizational commitment

13
Self-Storage Company

This appointment, like so many, was a referral – not from a financial institution in this case, but rather a request from an accountant acquaintance to 'help out' a family company.

What had happened was that the business had been built up over some thirty years by a buccaneering type of entrepreneur doing 'a bit of this, a bit of that' with a marginally discernible thread of cohesion but without much in the way of strategy for managing or developing the company in the context of commercial logic. Basically it was in bulk storage – grain and the like, and deriving excellent returns from EC Intervention storage – but it had diversified along the way into small-scale plant hire on the one hand (initially fork-lifts and similar items, but later also cranes) and into machinery movement on the other. The company's founder had a large family, of which he let three sons into the business – but he neglected to give them any relevant training, neither did he allow them any authority or responsibility. Suddenly and prematurely, he died, and the three sons (all in their twenties) turned to the company's auditor for help; he, realizing that what they needed was not so much financial assistance as an injection of management expertise, asked D. if he could get involved. The sons themselves understood that they needed outside help, and after the briefest of introductions and assessments they were content to go along with their auditor's recommendation and accept D. onto the board as non-executive chairman.

Well, what a shambles confronted D. on his arrival. The three sons in the business had each been 'given' his own division to run (without, as mentioned above, having been given any training as to *how* to go about doing this) but nobody had the remotest idea which activities were profitable and which weren't, and there was no real notion of any structure of responsibility. A dream for any company doctor, you might think.

But a family company presents unique challenges, many of which tend to revolve round the relative specific gravities of blood and water, and you have to tread pretty carefully at least until you have sussed out where real power lies, and even then you have to understand what it is acceptable to say and what may be out of order. In this case, the widow was in the office several days per week, and it obviously wasn't politic for D. to sound off about the shortcomings of her recently deceased husband while trying to unravel the chaos he had left behind!

The first essential, as D. saw things, was to put in some rudimentary controls which would be sufficient to show the directors which parts of the business were making money and which were losing money: fortunately, the overall position seemed reasonably profitable, so there was less immediate pressure than there might otherwise have been.

A measure of a structure of some kind was clearly necessary as a context in which to do such an analysis. So D. identified the company as having three operating divisions, and nominated each of the brothers as being in charge of one of these divisions; onto this he then grafted a management accounting system which showed the gross contribution from each division. This was extremely rough and ready at first, handwritten and rounded to the nearest significant figure, but it was religiously produced by one of the brothers every month and examined and discussed in detail at the board meeting, and all of them treated it very seriously.

In due course it was discovered that only one part of the business was actually making any money, and it was effectively subsidizing the others. This was abundantly clear from the figures, but of course it was a family company and it turned out that it wasn't the eldest brother's division which was the profitable one. Fortunately, the other brother whose division was found to be unprofitable recognized the fact and agreed that they had little option but to divest of it. This was the plant hire division – its main problem was that it simply wasn't large enough to compete effectively with the big boys, locally and nationally. Hiring out fork-lift trucks by themselves does not bring in sufficient money, and if you're in crane hire you have to be able to offer both a range of sizes and plenty of cranes themselves if you are to be taken seriously and so get a worthwhile volume of sales. Utilization rates here were around 40 per cent for the cranes and around 30 per cent for the fork-lifts, and levels such as those weren't enough to cover the allocated proportion of the overheads even though most of the pieces of plant were fully written off. It was, moreover, clear that they would be unable to steal business from the big operators without a level of marketing expenditure which was far beyond their resources.

So the decision was taken to sell the plant, and that's what they did. In fact, the sale raised considerably more cash than the directors had expected, which was later to prove most useful to the company. The brother whose division it had been then joined the brother in the profitable division, carving out a sales role for himself and thereby boosting its performance further.

Meanwhile, however, agreement on the other unprofitable division proved harder to come by. Despite the losses month after month, the eldest brother insisted that he could make it pay, and a family row was clearly looming. In fact, in the end he brought about his own downfall. At one month's board meeting, he turned up and announced that he had done absolutely nothing since the previous meeting 'just to show everybody how much money would be lost if that division weren't there!' D. lost his temper (something he rarely did, but when he did so he made it fairly spectacular) and scathingly criticized the eldest brother at the meeting, even though he was well aware of the risk of the three of them perhaps closing ranks against the outsider. Fortunately the other two brothers recognized the stupidity of the eldest's position, and backed D. The upshot was that 'his' division was handed over to him as an independent business for him to run without risk to the main company, and he very soon discovered the realities of life in a non-viable company. Even though he was given a cash float to start with, he was unable to make his business pay, and after a few months he had to accept the inevitable and close it down. Some time after this he dropped out of the company, and although still nominally a director he ceased to attend board meetings, instead seeking his fame and fortune somewhere else.

Meanwhile, the other two brothers (fortunately) grew rapidly in stature and maturity, and built on the rationalized business that was left after the divestment. This was the storage business; around the time of D.'s joining, they had diversified from bulk storage into self-storage, a relatively new concept in the UK though established in the United States. Basically it consisted of providing secure storage space, in units of various sizes, over which the customer had complete control in the sense that he held the key and could come and go as he pleased and could store more or less what he liked in any way he liked for whatever period he liked. Typical clients were, for example, families in the process of moving house, with a short-term need to store possessions between vacating one house and taking possession of the next, people perhaps off to work abroad for a spell, and so on.

The business was a good cash generator, and although there had been a cost associated with setting up the eldest brother in 'his' business, the company as a whole fairly quickly recovered from that and began to accumulate substantial cash reserves. The approach D. had implemented with regard to monthly financial reporting proved reasonably robust, and they were able to adapt it, with the help of the auditors acting as financial advisers, for use in financial modelling to enable the board to appraise certain policy options in seeking to grow the business further. They looked at the possibility of an expansion in another city, but when they were quite near to a deal the asking price suddenly altered, and the financial model was able to tell them that the prospect was no longer attractive.

Shortly after, an opportunity arose for expansion nearer home, and thanks to their cash 'war chest' they were able to take advantage of the opportunity and go for the expansion. Early results from the newly-expanded operation were a bit disappointing, but the financial projections suggested that things would come good, and that was in fact what happened after the first year. By now the two brothers were firmly in control of the business, and the systems were mature and stable. D. was no longer in a position to add any real value, so by mutual agreement he came off the board, just over four years after first joining the company. He subsequently received a really nice letter of thanks from the directors, saying that the company would not have got to where it was without his input. It doesn't by any means always happen that a non-exec gets such a vote of thanks for what he has done, but when it does happen it certainly makes things seem worthwhile. The company is still very much in operation, and seems to have prospered and expanded further since.

Looking at this case, there was an element of D.'s being in the right place at the right time. The untimely death of the company's founder opened up an opportunity which landed in his lap, and it so happened that he could provide more or less exactly what was being sought. Moreover, although the company exhibited many of the characteristics of childhood, and indeed of infancy, there was a profitable operation at the heart of the business, so it could be argued that all that was required was to identify where the profitability was, and then go for it.

However, the key to success undoubtedly lay in D.'s riding his piece of luck and creating an environment in which that could all happen. As in many families, the brothers fought like cats and dogs at times, and part of D.'s role as the outside director in a family company was to hold the metaphorical coats while they did so, conscious the whole time that it was always perfectly possible they would suddenly have a fit of solidarity and turn on him instead of each other! An objective summary of his contribution would be that initially he took a leadership role and in doing so injected a sufficient amount of thinking, professionalism, system and focus into the company to create a stable base and give the future managers time to develop their own expertise so that they could then take over and carry it on to further success. He used his networking resources from time to time to help to generate sales opportunities and set up other useful contacts, he did his share of mentoring, and he performed both as a thinker and as a doer. Overall, the contribution D. made does not perhaps appear as particularly spectacular, but it quite clearly guided the enterprise through its formative stages to a kind of maturity, and is perhaps representative of the kind of contribution that is repeated many times over in SMEs where an effective non-exec is on the board. And there is little doubt that it is all the more valuable and hard-won where the company is family-owned and family-managed.

Summary of key points

Stage of company's evolution: Childhood

Role/s played by non-exec: Leader
                                  Mentor
                                  Thinker
                                  Doer
                                  Evaluator
                                  Networker

Competencies required: **Thinking**   - all

                             Getting results   - Initiative
                                                   - Results focus
                                                   - Thoroughness
                                                   - Critical information
                                                     seeking
                                                   - Concern for
                                                     efficiency
                                                   - Developing
                                                     people

Influencing	- Interpersonal awareness
	- Concern for impact
	- Persuasiveness
	- Organizational awareness
	- Situational sensitivity
Self-managing	- Independence
	- Self-development
	- Positive self-image
	- Flexibility
	- Organizational commitment

14
Conclusions

It is clear from the case histories in Chapters 6–13 that a successful spell as a non-executive director in an SME may entail most or all of the roles and competencies previously discussed, whatever the stage of its evolution a particular company has reached.

Not all non-executive directorships are ever likely to be as interesting, stimulating or challenging as the eight described, but they all have the potential to give rise, to a greater or lesser degree, to situations and demands of the types illustrated by those case studies. It may only be a single incident, rather than a whole stream of things; it may only be a 'mild dose' of some problem, rather than a full-blown crisis; it may be something where the particular set of skills on offer is not necessarily uniquely valuable, and possibly a different individual in the non-exec seat might have acted in some other way and there might have been a different outcome! At the end of the day the identity of the particular individual in that seat is going to be significant in relation to the action and the outcome, but probably not in relation to the situation itself. The non-exec's seat at the board table in the examples described was usually a pretty hot seat – surprisingly so, and hotter than you might expect in the abstract. It was also (significantly) hotter, and hotter for more of the time, than would be usual in a large organization.

For it should by now be apparent that although there are common areas of responsibility and attention for non-executive directors across the entire spectrum of organization types and sizes, it is the strong contention here that the small and medium-sized enterprise sector offers a quite particular set of demands and priorities to be faced by non-execs. Few would nowadays argue with the notion that the area of 'governance' is a prime focus for non-exec attention, capitalizing not only on the non-exec's ability to stand a little way back and observe dispassionately and critically how the organization is directed and managed, but also on the likelihood of his having a relatively wide experience base and a high level of maturity, and being able to draw on both of those to make comparisons and judgements. But whereas in a larger organization 'governance' may well be the principal or even the only aspect to which the non-exec is expected to make a significant contribution, in a smaller organization that is not necessarily the case, and the relative shortage of senior management and directorial experience or capability makes it extremely likely that a more hands-on contribution will be required for at least part of the time.

It was earlier asked whether there was a 'universal' SME non-executive director, and the thread of argument seemed to be moving towards the conclusion that there was not, though there was clearly a significant number of common threads linking the various activities of those upon whom such a model (if it could be defined) might be based. Now it is important to avoid being too prescriptive, largely because things change so quickly that today's prescription can easily become tomorrow's anachronism, and one should beware of those authorities who would have books such as this set out a kind of A to Z of how to be an SME non-exec. At the same time, however, it must be acknowledged that having drawn attention at the very opening of the book to the absence of such a teaching aid, it would perhaps be evading the issue then to look at competencies and roles and not pass any opinions on their relevance.

A number of things have been attempted in this book. First, I have tried to identify the key elements of a contemporary non-executive director's function, and then tried to set that in the particular context of SMEs. An attempt has been made to distil the 'essence' of what the SME non-exec's contribution actually is (or what it could or should be) and to put that into some kind of codification or framework in which it might be more readily recognized and therefore evaluated and optimized. An attempt has been made to show, based on genuine experience, some of the kinds of things which real-life SME non-execs get asked to do and to get involved in, highlighting aspects which make these things peculiar to SMEs – and, of course, in doing so to illustrate how precarious an SME's hold on life can be and how the wheels may fall off even when people are working to their utmost and beyond and are not necessarily doing anything markedly wrong or inappropriate. In doing these things, I have tried to offer as objective a view as possible of the validity and/or relevance of the various models, theories, preferences and behaviour patterns that have been encountered.

The question that has occurred over and over again during the writing of this book, and no doubt to many SME non-execs in the course of their work, is along the lines of 'is it worth it?' Does it *work* to have non-execs in SMEs, does anyone gain anything out of it, or is it all something of a mare's nest, something which seems to have some sense and substance but turns out actually, when you get to it, to be illusory?

The key reason why this particular question recurs and is so central to the principles and experiences written about here has a lot to do with the fundamental irony of SMEs – they are the type of organization perhaps most in need of what an effective non-exec can deliver, and yet at the same time they are also perhaps the least able to afford an effective non-exec or to capitalize properly on what he *can* deliver. The issue of added-value was considered earlier and the clear view expressed that a non-exec must, like any other labourer, be worthy of his hire. But people will variously express, from time to time, sentiments like 'the level of reward an SME can offer is not going to attract sufficiently high-quality individuals', and 'it's only too easy to over-estimate what a non-exec can actually achieve in the face of small thinking, or perhaps just indifference, or even perhaps plain muddle and incompetence, on the part of the executives'.

Such a point of view is entirely understandable. Indeed, it will have been clear from some of the case studies described in Part II that non-execs themselves are far from immune to their share of frustration and disappointment, not to say disillusionment. But it would be too simple, and indeed simplistic, to take refuge in that and to ignore the wider issues which come into play; issues which quite clearly apply just as much in management as in any other areas of life. For example, people who are good at something don't generally do it *only* for the financial reward – part, at least, of their reward comes from the satisfaction of achievement and the knowledge of having achieved. Equally, people who are good at something are usually 'in' it for the long term, and tend to accept short-term frustrations as part and parcel of what is entailed in what they do. They are creative in terms of the way they cope with these frustrations, and this very creativeness helps, in fact, to make them even more effective at whatever it is they are involved in.

Indeed, creativeness should be high on the list of essential attributes for the effective SME non-executive director. It is what makes flexibility a distinguishing competency, and it is what can make an effective thinker an effective doer as well. It is a real 'driver' for change and development within organizations – firstly because creativeness and change are to an extent almost synonymous, and secondly because you often find people extremely resistant to change not because of some deep-rooted bloody-mindedness but rather as the result of a weariness at having seen it happen so many times before with usually limited, if any, lasting benefit arising from it. To have any realistic prospect of capturing the hearts and minds of such people, to kindle an enthusiasm for the maturing process, you have to bring something fresh, perhaps unusual or unexpected, to the party, and this is undoubtedly where creativeness scores, not only in the context of policies and plans but also in terms of the everyday things you say and do.

But 'the everyday things?' Are there actually such elements in SME non-execs' lives? Certainly, there are some reasonably well-defined basic responsibilities and functions (see, for example, the 3i 'specification' reproduced in Chapter 1) and there is no doubt that there are non-execs in all sizes and types of organizations who do no more than dutifully fulfil those responsibilities and functions and who consider themselves effective, hoping their colleagues agree with that consideration. On the other hand, if one is asked to describe what an effective SME non-exec *does*, one can rattle fairly easily through the territory highlighted by 3i – guidance, confidential advisor, boardroom priorities, strategy and plans, objective views on performance, corporate legislation, outside experience, and use of external contacts – but then one really needs to add words to the effect of 'mucking in as and when required to help with more or less any aspect of the business in which you have knowledge or capability'. The eight directorships described in Chapters 6–13 were in fact pretty typical of those with which the author himself has had any involvement, and one of the characteristics common to all of them was the high level of unpredictability. Certainly there have been occasions when the non-exec has had a troubleshooting role specified pretty well from the start, and as such could predict at least some of the things he would subsequently get involved in, but on the whole the best advice would appear to be to expect the unexpected and be prepared to cope with it, while at the same time remembering that there is usually an ongoing boardroom agenda (of which you must be part) around managing an organization and trying to get it to change, develop and mature.

As I have tried to show, the reality is that it *is* possible to bring about real change and real development even in small organizations, and to make those changes and developments take root. And it may be argued that achieving this goes a very long way towards making up for the times when for whatever reason it isn't achieved, and that the times when it goes right make everything worthwhile.

But it's obviously not easy to get it right, so how should we go about it? Will we even recognize when it is right?

The most essential thing is to recognize that there aren't many absolutes, if indeed any at all. Like the rhinestone cowboy, celebrated in song,
who had to do a load of compromisin' on the road to his horizon, the SME
non-exec has to play a lot of his situations by ear. It has been suggested
that SMEs tend to live their lives nearer the edge, as it were, than larger
companies, and that their executives can spend much of their time in
a state of near-panic. As far as the author's experience and observation
suggest, this is quite simply a fact of life; it may not be particularly
desirable, nor perhaps conducive to the exercise of sound management
principles, but there is, arguably, an element of inevitability about it.
It is attributable to a combination of many circumstances – shortage of
management skills and experience, inadequacy of working capital, short-
termism on the part of institutional lenders, to name a few of the more
obvious ones. Every now and again, perhaps, a 'star' comes along and
shoots through the SME phase on its way to being something much
bigger and grander, but the vast majority of SMEs never in fact become
anything other than SMEs. For this majority, the reality of day-to-day
life lies in a constant struggle – to find business, to perform and deliver
what has been won, to juggle priorities, and to get cash in quickly enough
to fund what has to be paid out – and in that struggle, it is sometimes
simply not possible to preserve ideological purity in the sense of putting
sound management principles into practice. On occasions, customer
goodwill has to be abused, loyal employees have to be exploited, some
creditors have to be given artificial preference over others, those providing
funds have to be given information the accuracy of which cannot be
absolutely guaranteed, and promises which come very close to being
fraudulent are issued (to the accompaniment of much crossing of corporate fingers).

Put like that, it sounds horrific. However, if you think about it objectively for a moment, what it surely amounts to is no more than the
essential to-ing and fro-ing of daily business, a totality of processes which
is also found in large organizations but which is not usually so sharply-
focused there as in smaller bodies where everything is much more
visible. It must also have been apparent from the case studies analysed
that what is actually achieved 'on the ground' is frequently (indeed one
might say 'usually') some way away from what any textbook solution
would prescribe, and must appear almost inferior beside such textbook
solutions. But the point that is really being made is this: a non-exec in
such an environment who cannot live with what is going on in real life,
whose high moral ground is *so* high that it's out of the sight of ordinary
mortals, is frankly wasting his time, as well as that of his executive

colleagues. This is not the first book, and it certainly won't be the last, to suggest that management is 'the art of the possible', and the immediacy of the world of the SMEs highlights this truism. Being a non-exec in an SME is no less the art of the possible, because of the ready involvement of non-execs in the SME's management. Sweeping swarf off the floor and using the proceeds from its sale to pay the wages, out of sight of the trade creditors and the bank, isn't the kind of thing you will find in most books about management, but it worked in the circumstances.

Hold on a minute, though, you may say. Wasn't there great stress laid earlier on the need for a coherent value system, for some clarity as to where you the non-exec stand, and doesn't that give rise to a potential conflict with the notion of fleet-footedness and an ability to compromise or to find novel solutions to problems?

The answer, of course, is yes. That conflict, and the ability to resolve it or at least to reconcile aspects of it, lies at the very heart of being a director, and in particular of being a director of an SME. If you can't move in the direction of resolution or reconciliation, you won't be much use to your SME; if you can't even recognize the conflict, you won't be any use at all. Reconciliation or resolution nearly always requires some compromise, some willingness to step down from one's pedestal and mix things with one's colleagues or opposite numbers, and this doesn't have to be a sign of weakness or defeatism. The competencies highlighted in Chapter 3 and the roles discussed in Chapter 4 are all about what it takes to square the circle of boardroom principle-and-practice in SMEs. Bear in mind that that swarf swept up off the factory floor did in fact safeguard the interests of the trade creditors and the bank because it allowed the company to continue operating and thus to generate further funds. So if you are in some way and at some time effective, it's worth it. It doesn't mean to say that the business necessarily has a long-term future – it can be argued that there is no guarantee of that anywhere nowadays – but it does mean to say that the touchstone is whether, and to what extent, and within reason for how long, the business is the better for your input. And 'better' means not necessarily just more profitable, but more under control, more able to meet its objectives and obligations, in contemporary parlance more 'sorted'. A company that isn't 'sorted' will have a much smaller chance of making it through to maturity and the stability that state may bring.

How, then, finally, should that input be delivered? Most importantly, on the basis of a thorough-going professionalism. A non-exec, even if his hands are fairly far 'off', is part of an organization's management, and there should be no doubt at all that management should be regarded as a profession every bit as much as, say, teaching, accountancy, law or medicine. There may have been a place at one time (though I personally am far from convinced) for the 'gifted amateur' in management, but there certainly isn't now. The stakes are too high for the field to be left open to a wide range of abilities. More or less every aspect of human endeavour is becoming increasingly competitive, as access improves and widens, and of course increasingly transparent and measurable, and those who are visibly unable to make the grade cannot realistically expect to be given serious consideration alongside those who really tackle the challenges in a mature and integrated way. This kind of approach is pretty generally accepted in the context of managers and executive directors, especially in larger organizations, but it's by no means certain that as a theory it yet underpins the transactions of SMEs and in particular of non-executives in them.

But in the final analysis, executive or non-executive, it matters not – as surely as the sun rises and sets, your colleagues and stakeholders will recognize and reward high-quality and professional performance and will just as surely punish the poor quality and amateurish. In a small organization, there is less room to hide if individual performance is not up to scratch; as has been noted more than once, as an SME non-exec you are quite likely to be in a cohort of one in your organization, and that spells 'exposure'. If you are not happy with that, don't do it, for you would be travelling along the wrong route.

Managing an SME is certainly no bed of roses, and for every small business that becomes a 'star' there are hundreds, probably thousands, of others whose directors wonder why they ever bothered! Being a non-executive director of an SME is not something to be undertaken lightly or wantonly, either. It is a job, a job that's worth doing and therefore worth doing well, and whilst hopefully it has been demonstrated here that it takes a fairly special type of individual to make an effective SME non-exec, hopefully it has also been demonstrated that as a breed they are not pretending to be superhuman. What they offer – or what it is suggested they ought to offer – is a set of recognizable attributes and skills that can be isolated from the sets offered by others and can be matched to recognizable needs. That matching process is a significant responsibility on non-execs themselves, on host SMEs, and on those who in some way broker the relationships. It is a process which appears so far to have been inadequately researched and understood, and it is hoped that this work may make some contribution towards rectifying that situation.

Summary of key points

- The demands placed upon the non-executive director of an SME are very wide-ranging and not confined to issues of governance. It is very likely that a number of different roles will require to be assumed, irrespective of the stage a particular company has reached in its evolution. Equally, it appears that the majority of the competencies identified as necessary for non-exec success are required in a majority of instances.
- It is also very likely that a degree of hands-on involvement will be required at some time during a non-exec's period of office.
- An attempt has been made in this book to show real examples of how and where that hands-on involvement may be called for.
- There is a fundamental irony in the need for non-exec input being most needed by the types of companies that may be least able to afford it. However, it should be noted that really effective non-execs are not 'in it' solely for the money.
- Effective non-execs possess a significant amount of creativeness, which tends to enhance their competencies and the extent to which they succeed in their roles. It also helps them to foster and lead a process of change and development within their organisations.
- It is also essential for an effective SME non-exec to be sufficiently realistic to understand when to stick rigidly to, and when to compromise on, management principles. The ability to resolve (or at least reduce) the conflict between maintaining recognized standards and finding novel and imaginative solutions to problems is key to being effective as a director, particularly in an SME. An essential criterion is whether or not a non-exec has, by his input, made a business better able to cope with the present and the possible future.
- There is less and less room for the amateur in management – and this applies equally to executives and non-executives. Competition and accountability mean that only those who are genuinely competent will be recognized as successful, and the smaller the organization the greater the extent of individual exposure to scrutiny.
- SME non-execs should not be expected to be superhuman, but the best of them should be able to offer something special in the way of skills and attributes. Matching these to what SME's really need is a major responsibility, and a process that has some way still to develop.

Notes and References

1. *Making it Happen: Reflections on Leadership* by Sir John Harvey-Jones (London, Collins: 1988) is written very much as a reflection on how he has reacted to the situations he has faced since his days in the navy in the immediate aftermath of World War II, and how he has developed an approach and a style of leadership. His definitions and criteria do not claim to be particularly original, but they are backed up by the evidence of his own achievements, especially during his period as Chairman of ICI (1982–7).
2. *Directors' Dilemmas* by Patrick Dunne (London, Kogan Page: 2000) is a highly readable work drawing from what he has seen, heard and done as an executive with 3i, and in particular as head of their Independent Director programme. It focuses on situations which directors may meet, and choices they may have to make in dealing (or not dealing) with those situations, and tries to establish principles as well as looking at a number of case studies based around actual experiences of directors and commenting upon how they were tackled by those involved.
3. This is largely anecdotal, and as a statistic not particularly robust; as an indicator of a trend, however, it has some validity, and may be corroborated by sampling from companies' annual returns.
4. The Committee on the Financial Aspects of Corporate Governance was set up under the chairmanship of Sir Adrian Cadbury and reported in December 1992 (published by Gee). Its establishment was probably to some extent a reaction to public and (especially) media outcry over the rewards given to, and gains netted by, some of the top managers of the utilities which had been privatized during Margaret Thatcher's period as Prime Minister – particularly in cases where a privatized utility was perceived as performing badly in service or value-for-money terms. However, it would be unfair to characterize the Committee's birth and work as merely a knee-jerk reaction, for there was at that time an increasing understanding in business and public life of the need for accountability, albeit sometimes imperfectly articulated and presented in terms mainly of tabloid headline-style reports!

    The Committee's work and pronouncements were highly influential and contributed to a greatly increased sense of the importance of accountability and transparency in board proceedings. Over the ensuing few years, there were several other committees which sat considering other aspects of corporate governance such as executive remuneration and stock exchange rules, and the sum total of their contribution to improved corporate behaviour has been fairly considerable. (See next three notes.)
5. Sir Richard Greenbury's Study Group looked into directors' remuneration, and reported in July 1995. Its main output was a Code of Best Practice based on principles of accountability, in which the requirement for listed companies to have a remuneration committee was enshrined and given the status almost of a statute.

6. Sir Ronald Hampel chaired the Committee on Corporate Governance, which delivered its report in January 1998. The thrust of its recommendations was primarily towards a kind of 'formalization' in the way listed companies approached the issue of corporate governance and towards the promotion of greater openness and transparency in the way they put its principles into practice.

7. By the time Derek Higgs was asked by the Secretary of State for Trade and Industry to carry out his *Review of the Role and Effectiveness of non-Executive Directors*, in 2002, questions had begun to be asked about the effectiveness of the 'watchdog' role traditionally ascribed to non-execs. Specifically, there was a growing perception that they had proved somewhat toothless in the face of a trend towards massive reward packages being given to chief executives of companies that were seen to fail – perhaps the most spectacular example was Marconi, where the chief executive who had presided over the almost total collapse of what had once been the mighty GEC walked away with a seven-figure severance package. Higgs' report, published in January 2003, was greeted by the media with a certain amount of puzzlement about whether it would actually have any impact on the way such 'deals' happened, and by the corporate sector variously with howls of anguish about the wedges being driven between executive and non-executive directors, and some more sober reflections on the possible need for business to put its own house in order before someone else tried to do it for them.

8. The *Marchioness* was a Thames pleasure boat. On the night of 20 August 1989, 51 people at a party on board were killed when it was in collision with a dredger, the *Bow Belle*. Although eventually a decision was taken not to prosecute anyone, on the apparent grounds that actually proving culpability would be extremely difficult, if not impossible, the inquiry into the disaster took some two years and there was considerable speculation about possible prosecutions.

9. In March 1993 four teenagers were drowned in a canoeing accident in Lyme Bay, Dorset. They were taking part in an activity holiday organised by a local outdoor activities centre. The Managing Director of the centre was prosecuted, convicted of manslaughter, and jailed, while the company running the centre was convicted of 'corporate manslaughter' and fined £60,000.

10. Taken from *The Independent Director*, published by Director Publications Ltd and Kogan Page (1999). This booklet is one of a series in a joint initiative by the Institute of Directors and Ernst & Young comprising workshops, publications, and events, all aimed at clarifying the role, interests and needs of non-executive directors. It examines these from a number of different perspectives – that of the SME, of the PLC, and of the institutional investor – in a clear and concise way, though hitherto the attention paid to the particular situation of the SME has been relatively scant.

11. 3i maintain details of a cohort of individuals for nomination as non-executive members of boards of investee companies. In the late 1980s this was formalized on a UK-wide basis and christened their 'Independent Director Resource'. Regionally-based meetings of the Resource take place from time to time at various of 3i's local offices, and the Resource is in some localities a thriving network. The author was a member of the Resource for some fifteen years.

12. *The Cadbury Report*, page 21, para. 4.12

13. *The Independent Director* (1999)

14. *The Stock Exchange Combined Code* seeks to regulate the conduct of quoted companies by setting down standards and protocols covering the way companies and their boards of directors should carry out their functions. Although it does not itself have the force of law, it can institute action, and apply sanctions, against companies which breach the code; and in practice such breaches would in fact also contravene one or more of the relevant acts of parliament.

15. *The Role and Contribution of an Independent Director*, a small booklet produced by 3i in the 1980s, for use principally by their investee companies and by non-execs appointed to boards in those companies.

16. The post of Commissioner for Public Appointments was created in November 1995 on the recommendation of the Nolan Committee, which had been set up to examine concerns about standards in public life. Dame Rennie Fritchie DBE is the current holder of the post: as commissioner she is independent of both government and the civil service, and regulates and monitors appointments made by ministers to all non-departmental public bodies and health bodies, as well as those of the utility regulators. There is a code of practice governing all these appointments, based on seven principles including the need to pursue equal opportunities policies and the practice of making appointments based solely on merit.

17. It should be noted that since 2000 the structure of many NHS bodies has begun to change, with a move towards fewer non-executive members but greater representation from various interest groups within, and connected with, the Health Service. It seems likely that this process is far from over: there is significant opposition within the Labour party to the whole idea of NHS Trusts, so it is entirely possible that some other form of organization may be developed to replace these. Whether, and if so on what basis, any replacement organizations may have non-executive input is of course completely open to question – though not to have it would seem to fly somewhat in the face of currently accepted governance thinking and practice.

18. Statistics published by the Department of Trade and Industry.

19. The problems were identified in a survey carried out for the National Westminster Bank and commented upon in *Management Matters* (March 1999) in an article highlighting the Small Firms Enterprise Development Initiative.

20. A study carried out by the accountants Stoy Hayward in 1992, and quoted in *The Economist* in October of that year, suggested that 24 per cent survived into the second generation and 14 per cent into the third. More recently, the author has been told anecdotally that the figures are 30 per cent and 10 per cent. Since any study is going to be based on a sample, it seems probable that the reality lies in a range, and that the somewhat imprecise figures quoted in the text are sufficient to make the essential point about the fall-off rate after the first generation.

21. *What Makes an Effective Independent Director – Competency Research Study* by Boardroom Development Ltd (1998). This study, carried out in collaboration with the University of Sheffield, looked at the factors contributing to high performance in the boardrooms of UK companies and organizations and into the competencies or behaviours associated with success in the independent director role. It is analysed and discussed here by permission.

22. The methodology of this piece of research was interesting and, it seemed to me, quite robust in that there appeared to be very little in the way of value judgement on the part of the researchers in what was essentially a qualitative exercise. One assumes that those non-execs who took part were honest in the accounts they gave of their thoughts and actions, in which case there was a remarkable congruity among them all in how they had reacted to and tackled difficult situations, and the only value-related input from the researchers was in devising forms of words which covered manifestations of the same competencies. Hence the comment about what the non-exec sees in the mirror.

23. Warren Bennis, American psychologist, professor, leadership 'guru', and sometime presidential adviser, wrote several books on leadership over a twenty-year period (1970s to 1990s). His identification of four key competencies for leadership, later modified into four 'new rules' – providing direction and purpose, generating and sustaining relationships based on trust, leaning towards action even though this might mean taking risks, and radiating hope and optimism and the expectation of success – earned him wide recognition and respect among management thinkers and consultants. He is also noteworthy for his advocacy of a degree of humility on the part of a leader.

24. *A Force for Change* by John P. Kotter (New York, Free Press: 1990). Since the early 1980s, Kotter has amassed an impressive volume of casework in his studies of organizational behaviour and leadership. Like Bennis (q.v.) he distinguishes between 'leadership' and 'management', but unlike Bennis he sees leadership not just in 'leaders' themselves but in whole organizations – within organizations, acts of leadership may occur at almost any level and may involve entire teams of people.

25. *Management of Organizational Behavior: utilizing human resources* by Paul Hersey and Kenneth H. Blanchard (London, Prentice-Hall, 1st edn: 1969). A highly influential book which built upon earlier work by management scientists such as Maslow and Herzberg in the fields of motivation. The extent of popularity and influence achieved by this work may perhaps be gauged by the fact that it is now in its seventh edition (1996).

26. Max Weber (1864–1920), a lawyer and political economist, was an early writer on management theory who distinguished 'authority' from 'power' and identified three distinct types of the former – traditional, where people obey someone in authority specifically because he is in a position of authority (for example, in a hereditary type of system); charismatic, where people obey because of an individual's personal qualities (and where there is always a danger that things will fall apart once that charismatic individual is no longer there), and rational, where people fit into a pattern of hierarchy and bureaucracy, and what they do is pre-specified and laid out in such a way as to minimize scope for personal initiative. Weber saw the rational-type organization as being in most respects the best model in terms of effectiveness and efficiency, whereas he saw the other two as vulnerable to the whims – and possible mistakes – of those in authority. He also predicted that organizations run on the basis of charismatic authority would (as it were) mutate over time into one of the other two types. Although influential for a while, Weber's ideas have tended to fall out of favour as more modern management thinkers place more emphasis on individuals' roles and choices

within organizations: however, an analysis of the ways in which authority is derived and exercised in organizations today, can still show a great deal of validity in Weber's observations and descriptions.

27. From an article in *The Director* magazine, March 1996.
28. Research by the University of Paisley and the Centre for Leadership Studies, University of Surrey, reported on in an article entitled 'Boardroom Leadership: Do Small and Medium Companies Need Non-Executive Directors?' by Patrick Mileham in the *Journal of General Management*, Vol. 22, No. 1, Autumn 1996.

Index